HIDDEN
HISTORY
of
PRESCOTT

Parker Anderson

THE
History
PRESS

Published by The History Press
Charleston, SC
www.historypress.com

First published 2021

Manufactured in the United States

ISBN 9781467146807

Library of Congress Control Number: 2021934132

Notice: The information in this book is true and complete to the best of our knowledge. It is offered without guarantee on the part of the author or The History Press. The author and The History Press disclaim all liability in connection with the use of this book.

To my friend Fred Hamilton of North Myrtle Beach, South Carolina,
who passed away while this book was being written.
He would have enjoyed this work very much. Roads go ever, ever on…

Contents

ACKNOWLEDGEMENTS

Special thanks to Brenda Taylor and the staff of Sharlot Hall Museum Library and Archives for continuing to allow me access to their holdings as I work to bring out the lesser-known stories and facts about Prescott and Yavapai County in my books. I am extremely grateful to Darlene Wilson of Haunted Prescott Tours for assisting me in the graphics and layout for this book. Thanks to Laurie Krill of The History Press for giving me the opportunity to write this book. A big shout-out to my close friend Jody Drake, who has always supported me in my endeavors. Finally, thanks to the residents of my town of Prescott, Arizona, who have collectively not gotten too angry with me for debunking local legends over the years! (Big smile!)

INTRODUCTION

The city of Prescott, established in 1864, lies in central Arizona, surrounded by mountains and Ponderosa pine trees. It is a thriving metropolitan area with a population that exceeds forty-five thousand today (not counting the equally large neighboring city of Prescott Valley, nine miles east of Prescott, which was founded in 1966) and is expected to more than double that in the next twenty-five years. The growth of Prescott has been extraordinary in recent times, with the population having quadrupled just since 1980.

In the late nineteenth and early twentieth centuries, the chief source of Prescott's economy was mining, mostly copper. This was true of most inhabited Arizona communities in those early days. But there came a time, largely by the 1950s, when the mining started to die out. Many mining towns in Arizona evaporated and became ghost towns. Prescott survived, and today, its economy is based on tourism, retail and its reputation for being a beautiful city for retirement.

As it was the first real town established in the newly created Arizona Territory in 1864, much has been written about the history of Prescott over the years, with varying degrees of accuracy. Yet much of the early influences on the community have been largely ignored. Little has been written, for instance, on the history of the Yavapai Indian tribe, who were here first and were displaced by the white man until they were able to establish a reservation many years later. Likewise, much legend and rumor exist about Prescott's early Chinese immigrants, but to date, there has been only one serious attempt (the Lister study) to tell their history.

Fraternal organizations and secret society lodges have held strong influence in the history of Prescott. When the Arizona Territory was established, one of the first things the original governor's party felt it had to do was establish a branch of the Masonic Lodge. Then there were the once-revered but now-notorious Smoki People, who were a major power in town through much of the twentieth century. Their stories, as well as those of other secretive organizations in Prescott, will be told in these pages.

Finally, I have included a few personal favorite stories from Prescott's hidden history—stories that have not been repeated very often, such as the city's brush with strange UFO cults. If you think you have already read and heard everything about Prescott and its history, I think you will enjoy the ensuing pages very much.

YAVAPAI-PRESCOTT INDIAN TRIBE

The Yavapai are a Native American tribe in central Arizona. From their language, their name translates literally as "People of the Sun." Before the incursion of white settlers, miners and the military, the Yavapai occupied a vast region of land in what would become the Arizona Territory. Technically, before the Mexican War of 1846, Mexico claimed all of this land, but its citizens and officials seldom if ever explored this region, largely due to the heavy population of Native American tribes. Consequently, the tribes, who had been living in these regions since the beginning of time, considered the land to be theirs (and modern historians support this), and they were unaware that anyone else was technically claiming the area.

At some point in history, the Yavapai were divided into four separate bands who lived in different areas of their region. They were the Yavbe' (Northwestern Yavapai), Do:lkabaya (Western Yavapai), Guwevkabaya (Southeastern Yavapai) and Wi:pukba (Northeastern Yavapai—today the Yavapai tribe in the Verde Valley). They lived largely apart and considered themselves separate people.

The Yavapai had a lot in common with the Apache tribe and were often mistaken for them by the white man. In his memoirs, the once celebrated but now notorious "Indian fighter" General George Crook did not, or could not, distinguish between them, even though some of the battles he was involved in had to be with the Yavapai.

The first contacts with the Yavapai made by "outsiders" were modest. In 1583, the Spanish explorer Antonio de Espejo met the tribe when he came to the region looking for gold, led by Hopi guides. He reportedly met the tribe near the mountains of what is today the town of Jerome. In 1598, explorer Marcos Farfán de los Godos came to the area for the same reason, but neither explorer found gold. Also, in 1598, an exploring group led by the brutal Spanish conquistador Juan de Oñate passed through Yavapai lands.

Father Francisco Garces was a Spanish missionary who made four trips into these regions in the 1700s to establish contact with the Native tribes. His diary, under the date of November 8, 1775, notes a meeting with the "Yabipays"; he had traveled north with a small group of Yuma Indians and met the tribe. Later, Father Garces, mapping the region, made note of the area where the "Yabipays" lived.

In his writings, famed explorer/botanist Baron Alexander von Humboldt made references to the "Yabipays," but he had not visited the region. Humboldt was relying on the writings of Father Garces and other Spanish explorers.

In 1846, the United States went to war with Mexico over land in the belief that we were destined, as a great nation, to reach across the continent from the Atlantic Ocean to the Pacific. President James K. Polk called this Manifest Destiny.

When Mexico surrendered and signed the Treaty of Guadalupe Hidalgo on February 2, 1848, it was forced to turn over to the United States more than half of its national land, consisting of what is today Texas, New Mexico, Arizona, Nevada, the lower half of California and areas of Colorado and Wyoming. It was the single largest land acquisition in American history. More land was acquired from Mexico, between the Gila River and the Rio Grande, in the Gadsden Purchase of 1853.

Having acquired all of this new land, the United States did not seem to have an organized plan for how to explore, map or settle it, and so it let much of it lie there. The California gold rush of the 1850s brought many settlers to that area, and Texas was slowly being colonized. The land in between—Arizona and New Mexico—remained inhabited mostly by the various Native American tribes, including the four branches of the Yavapai.

But inevitably, incursions into the area by the white man became a reality. Explorers such as Charles Debrille Poston, Herman Ehrenberg, Pauline Weaver, Charles Genung and Antoine Leroux entered what is now Arizona for the purpose of mapping and/or settlement and mining. The U.S. government sent military troops in to explore the region, set up posts and assess the Indian tribes.

In 1853, a military expedition under Lieutenants Amiel Weeks Whipple and J.C. Ives came to the area for all of the above reasons. Antoine Leroux was their guide and told them that when he had explored the area in the late 1840s, he estimated the number of the Yavapai tribe at about two thousand and that they were scattered into roughly four groups across the region that had very little contact with each other.

When the Whipple-Ives military expedition made contact with the Yavapai tribe, it found them in a sickly and debilitated condition. The military detachment was told that a violent and contagious sickness had broken out possibly the summer before, which decimated the ranks of the tribe, as well as those of other Native American tribes (particularly the Mohave tribe) in what would later become Arizona. Pioneer settler Charles Genung would later repeat this story and speculated that the unidentified plague had spread to other tribes quickly due to various tribal members trying to flee to other areas—this led to hostility between the tribes.

Pauline Weaver, explorer and sometimes army scout and one of the first white men to visit the area, feared this hostility would spread as the white man continued to arrive in greater numbers. He and another white explorer, John Moss, attempted to negotiate a peace treaty between the various tribes, giving them areas of land that other tribes could not enter without permission. The Yavapai were given the large area around what is today Prescott. Weaver and Moss also asked them to promise to be friendly to any white men who would come into the area. As we know today, none of this worked out well.

(As a footnote, explorer John Moss would later become rather notorious for calling himself "Captain" when he possessed no such title and exaggerating many of his exploring adventures.)

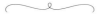

MORE WHITE MEN CAME to the region for mining, settling and ranching. The discovery of gold, copper and other valuable ore in the mountains of the region exacerbated the situation. On February 20, 1863, the U.S. Congress passed the Arizona Organic Act, officially creating the Territory of Arizona, and a first governor's party set out for the area to set up the new territorial government. Settling on the banks of Granite Creek, they founded the town of Prescott and proclaimed it the capital of the territory. Dividing the territory into four original counties, it reportedly was Pauline Weaver who suggested to the officials that the counties be named for Indian tribes. The four counties were named Mohave, Pima, Yuma and Yavapai.

The Indian Wars that affected all other areas of the Southwest where Native American tribes lived came to Arizona. As was the case in other areas, the white settlers, miners, military commands and government officials took by force any land they wanted, especially if it proved to have large amounts of ore. Indians fought back, and many depredations occurred on both sides. The newspapers of the era, including the *Arizona Miner* from Prescott, played up the attacks, blaming them fully on the "savages."

White people demanded that their government do something, so the U.S. military from nearby forts, such as Fort Whipple, combed the mountains and rounded up every tribal member they could find, and they were marched off to "reservations" the federal government had set up. Most of the Yavapai tribe had been captured by the early 1870s and was initially taken to the Yavapai–Apache Camp Verde Reservation. When the government closed that reservation in March 1875, 1,400 Yavapai were marched across the territory to the San Carlos Indian Reservation in southeastern Arizona. Reportedly, at least 375 of them died along the march.

The Indian reservations, controlled by the U.S. military in those days, were largely squalid prisons. White people viewed tribal members as animals and did very little to keep them supplied with food and medical care. By 1900, twenty-five years later, fewer than two hundred Yavapai remained on the San Carlos Reservation, most of them having died from disease and the squalid conditions there. With the Indian Wars pretty much over by this time, others had escaped the reservations and were living often isolated lives in remote areas and small towns.

By the time the Great Depression rolled around, many Yavapai had migrated back to the Prescott area, their once tribal homeland before the white man came. Prescott had grown into a solid, bustling small town by this time, but tribal members were having difficulty finding employment and homes to live in. When the Civil Works Administration (CWA) and Works Progress Administration (WPA) were formed to combat the Depression by strengthening the nation's infrastructure through construction and employment, the tribe and area civic leaders lobbied for funds to help the Yavapai.

CWA Project P43 was authorized to aid the Yavapai tribe in building homes in the area near the Fort Whipple Military Reservation (as it was known then). A Yavapai man named Sam Jimulla ("Red Ants") was put in charge of most of this construction, and houses of stone and concrete were built for Yavapai families. Sam Jimulla was becoming a respected leader of the Yavapai tribe in Prescott.

THE PASSING OF YEARS was changing the state of America's Indian reservations as well. They had begun as virtually a type of prison system operated by the U.S. military, with a commissioner of Indian affairs appointed to oversee them, where the various tribes were forced to live. But as time passed, the reservations were slowly (very slowly sometimes) coming to be recognized as autonomous regions, with the tribes exercising increasing control over the lands they had been placed on. But the Yavapai people in Prescott had no official reservation for themselves, and in the 1930s, they began lobbying the U.S. government for reservation land to be set aside for them in the Prescott area.

U.S. senator Carl Hayden (D-Arizona) lent his influence to the efforts, and Prescott civic leaders such as Grace Sparkes (from the Prescott Chamber of Commerce), Sharlot M. Hall (poet and former territorial historian) and Dr. Grace Chapman (daughter of Charles Genung) also supported the efforts.

Finally, on May 9, 1935, the U.S. government turned over seventy-five acres of land that belonged to Fort Whipple and created the Prescott Yavapai Indian Reservation. It was at that time the smallest reservation in America.

In those days yet, the commissioner of Indian affairs had the right under U.S. law to appoint the tribal leaders, and because of the work with the CWA project, he appointed Sam Jimulla as the local chief of the tribe. Jimulla was well liked enough by his people, though, that they held their own ceremony and elected him chief of the Yavapai tribe as well.

However, it did not last very long. Only five years later, in May 1940, Sam Jimulla was killed in a horseback riding accident. His wife, Viola, then succeeded him as chief of the Yavapai Tribe. This is significant, as Viola Jimulla was the first female chief of a North American Indian tribe and remains to this day one of the most revered figures in the history of the Yavapai-Prescott Indian Tribe.

VIOLA JIMULLA WAS BORN on the San Carlos Reservation circa 1878. She was named Sicatuva (meaning "Born Quickly") by her parents and was educated at the Indian Schools, first at the town of Rice, Arizona, and then at the Phoenix Indian School. The so-called Indian Schools were set up by the government to forcibly teach Native American children the "civilized" ways of the white man and to get them to forget their tribal ancestry. Today, this period is regarded as one of the most shameful episodes in American history. Sicatuva was enrolled under the name of Viola Pelhame (Pelhame being her stepfather's name); the name Viola probably came from the practice of anglicizing the students' names at the Indian Schools.

Reaching adulthood, Viola rejoined her family, who were by this time living on parts of the Fort Whipple Military Reservation near Prescott. It was here that she met Sam Jimulla, and they were married in 1901. They had five daughters, though only three lived to adulthood.

A convert to Christianity, Viola Jimulla was the first Yavapai tribe member to be baptized into the Presbyterian Church, and she worked diligently with Presbyterian missionaries to Native American tribes to build the first church for the Yavapai in 1922. She would attend many Christian conferences for Native Americans around the Southwest in the ensuing years.

In 1940, after the sudden passing of the Jimullas' adult daughter Amy, Sam Jimulla was killed in a riding accident, as previously noted, leaving Viola as chief of the tribe, a position she would hold until her death in 1966.

One of the things Viola Jimulla is remembered for as chief is her effort to bring the tribe into modern times. Under her, tribal members slowly adapted to contemporary dress instead of traditional Yavapai regalia. Increasing numbers of Yavapai were learning to speak English so they could get along in "town" (Prescott). The WPA homes that had been built for the tribe had running water and electricity, unlike other Indian reservations of the day.

A profile of Viola Jimulla in *Arizona Highways* stated that she kept a card index of all tribal members, with each receiving a monthly check from the tribe, the amount depending on how much work they had done. The article further reported that no dances were held by the tribe, owing to the chief's strong Christian beliefs. (At this time, many Christians believed that any form of dancing was sinful.)

In 1948, the Yavapai tribe sued the U.S. government for the land that had been forcibly taken from them in 1873, when they had been marched off to the San Carlos Reservation—the land that had been given to them in the treaty negotiated by Pauline Weaver. Eventually, in 1965, an Indian Claims Commission in Washington, D.C., ordered the United States to pay the tribe for the land at 1873 market value. Meanwhile, the government added 1,320 acres of land to the Prescott Yavapai Reservation in 1956.

In Prescott, Trinity Presbyterian Church had become one of the few integrated churches by the 1950s, with attendance by both white residents and Yavapai members. When the church successfully raised money for a

Viola Jimulla, chief of the Yavapai-Prescott Indian Tribe from 1940 to 1966, is seen weaving one of her famous baskets in this early 1960s photo. *Sharlot Hall Museum.*

Groundbreaking ceremonies for Trinity Presbyterian Church on Park Avenue in Prescott in 1960. Viola Jimulla, who was a member of the congregation, is seen in the foreground. *Sharlot Hall Museum.*

new, larger building on Park Avenue, Viola Jimulla (who had been very involved with the fundraising) gave a speech at the dedication ceremonies in 1960. Her children and grandchildren had long been active in the faith. Trinity Presbyterian Church still stands at 630 Park Avenue.

Viola Jimulla was a basket weaver. While many Native American women wove baskets, hers were unusually beautiful and well-crafted. She once said she gave most of them away and did not keep count of how many baskets she had woven. Shoots of cottonwood and mulberry trees were used for each basket's natural colors. Yavapai baskets often contain the symbols of stars, various animals and men, denoting the tribe's creation beliefs.

Today, Viola Jimulla's baskets are not easy to find. Surviving baskets not owned by the tribe are difficult to locate, owing to collectors' desire to hold on to them. The design of one of her baskets is used on the official Flag of the Yavapai-Prescott Indian Tribe.

Viola Jimulla died in 1966 at the age of eighty-eight and was buried at the tribal cemetery on the reservation next to her husband. She was succeeded as chief by her daughter Grace Mitchell, and upon Grace's death in 1976, Viola's other daughter, Lucy Miller, became chief until her death in 1984.

Following the death of Lucy Miller, the tribe reorganized and conferred its leadership responsibilities solely on the tribal president and the tribal council. For many years, Viola Jimulla's son-in-law Don Mitchell served as chair of the tribal council (1940–48) and then as president (1948–72). In 1972, her granddaughter Patricia Ann McGee became president (1972–88; 1990–94).

Grace Mitchell, daughter of Viola Jimulla, succeeded her mother as chief of the Yavapai-Prescott Indian Tribe and served from 1966 to 1976. This photo was taken in 1975. *Sharlot Hall Museum.*

Patricia McGee was a major influence on the tribe, possibly second only to her grandmother. She started applying for and obtaining federal grants for needed advancements on the reservation, including a community center. By the 1990s, McGee had secured millions of dollars in grant money to build a large resort and conference center on tribal land (the Prescott Resort, which was originally a Sheraton). It was under her leadership that the Yavapai Tribe leased reservation land for the Frontier Village shopping center, which drivers pass as they head toward Prescott on Highway 69.

The last few decades have solidified recognition of the Indian reservations as almost autonomous nations, not always subject to federal or state laws and regulations. Therefore, to raise needed funds, various tribes nationwide began opening casinos on reservation land in states where gambling is illegal. These Indian casinos have proven to be immensely popular with tourists and residents of nearby non-reservation towns. In 1992, Patricia McGee signed an Indian Gaming compact with the State of Arizona, and the tribe added a large casino to the Prescott Resort called Bucky's Casino. (This move led Sheraton to drop its sponsorship of the resort, but this seems to have not harmed the continued financial success of either the resort or the casino.) Another casino, Yavapai Casino, was added along Highway 69 later.

Patricia Ann McGee died on April 6, 1994, and was buried in the tribal cemetery with her family. Her untiring efforts to improve the economy of the Yavapai-Prescott Indian Tribe led her to be inducted into the Arizona Women's Hall of Fame in 2006. Her legacy, like that of her grandmother Viola Jimulla, continues to be felt by the tribe today.

The First—or Second—Capital

After acquiring all of that western land following the Mexican War and the Gadsden Purchase, the United States did not have a clear plan about what to do with it. In what would become Arizona, a small number of military posts were opened, such as Fort Whipple (named for General Amiel Weeks Whipple), located at Del Rio Springs, near what is today Chino Valley. These posts were the first settlements in Arizona and spent quite a bit of time in conflict with the various Indian tribes. Meanwhile, the Mexican settlement of Tucson remained sparsely inhabited and was the only real town in Arizona following the American occupation.

The first stray miners started coming in as well. In 1859, Charles D. Poston, with financing from New York brokers, set up a mining company at the old Mexican presidio of Tubac (abandoned when Mexico had to turn the land over to the United States following the Mexican War). Two years later, in 1861, however, the Civil War began, and many American troops were pulled out of this region to fight. Suddenly very vulnerable to Apache Indian attacks, Poston and his group were forced to flee.

Back in Washington, Poston and others began lobbying both Congress and President Abraham Lincoln to officially create the Territory of Arizona, thus giving the area all of the rights, duties and perks that any other American territory had.

On February 20, 1863, President Abraham Lincoln signed the Organic Act, creating the Territory of Arizona. This required him to appoint a slate of officials to send to the new territory and set up a government and a capital there. At the top of the list were Ohio congressman John Addison Gurley to be governor of the territory, New York journalist Richard C. McCormick to be secretary and Maine congressman John Noble Goodwin to be chief justice of the territorial supreme court. As a reward for his lobbying to create the Arizona Territory, Charles D. Poston was appointed to the relatively obscure position of superintendent of Indian affairs. Henry W. Fleury, a man of somewhat mysterious background from New York, was hired to be personal secretary to the governor. It should be presumed that McCormick, an established New Yorker, had recommended him.

Plans were upended when Gurley suddenly died from an attack of appendicitis, which was far less treatable in those days than it is today. A new governor would need to be appointed before the party could set out for the Arizona Territory. In a later article from the March 14, 1866 edition of the *Arizona Miner* (which Richard McCormick founded and owned after arriving in Arizona), McCormick recalled:

When John A. Gurley was made Governor of Arizona, he went often to the White House to talk over that country and its necessities. After receiving the appointment of Secretary of the Territory, I accompanied him. The President took a lively interest in the labor before us, and contributed in every way to our assistance, telling Mr. Gurley, jovially, that while he could not be expected to send an Army to Arizona, he would see that his scalp was properly protected. He went so far as to endorse the orders to military authorities and others upon our route, and in emphatic words requested them to be particular in their attentions. He was much interested in the reports from the mines, and said to one of our number: "Tell the miners I hope to visit them and dig some gold and silver after the war."

Upon the sudden death of Mr. Gurley, which he much deplored, I went with one of the judges of Arizona to ask the appointment of Mr. [John] Goodwin, then Chief Justice of the Territory to the vacancy. We were at the White House by 8 a.m., while William, the colored servant who had attended Mr. Lincoln from Springfield, was in the act of shaving him. He looked up, with his face white with lather, and said: "Is it the best judgment of you all [referring to the territorial officers] that Mr. Goodwin should be appointed?" Being told that it was, and that prompt action in the matter was important, that the starting of our party, already delayed, might not be seriously retarded, he said: "Well, see the members of the Cabinet, and we will try to fix it at the meeting at noon today." It was so fixed, and at two o'clock we had the new Governor's commission from the State Department.

When suggesting that the appointment of Mr. Goodwin would leave the Chief Justiceship of the Territory vacant, the President quickly said that he had a man for that place and begged that we would not name anyone. "It is Grimes' man," [referring to Senator Grimes of Iowa] *said he, "and I must do something for Grimes. I have tried hard to please him from the start, but he complains, and I must satisfy him if possible." And so, Grimes' man, Mr. Turner of Iowa, was made Chief Justice.*

That last paragraph was a dig at Chief Justice William F. Turner, depicting him as a beneficiary of political cronyism. Turner was disliked by McCormick and by other territorial officials.

The first governor's party traveled overland by coach—a very long journey. They were informally expected to set up the new Arizona capital at Tucson, the only sizable town in the territory, with a population of mostly Mexicans and some stray white men. On arriving in the territory in December 1863, Governor Goodwin was informed by General James H. Carleton that Tucson was a wild place and believed to be a hotbed of Confederate sympathizers. (The Civil War was still raging at this time.)

Once in the new territory, the party made a short stop at Navajo Springs, read aloud the territorial proclamation and officially swore in the government officers. They then proceeded on to Fort Whipple, at Del Rio Springs, to stop and rest and get their bearings and decide what to do. Should they proceed to Tucson despite the warnings? Should they stay at Fort Whipple and make that the capital? Or should they move on and try to find another spot?

After much scouting and debating, they moved farther south of Fort Whipple and stopped by the banks of Granite Creek. This area was inhabited by only a few stray miners and settlers, but the Arizona territorial officials decided this was the place to establish Arizona's capital. (The perceived prospect of gold mining in the surrounding area was an added inducement.) It was here that the first territorial legislature was convened. They enacted the laws of the territory, the counties were divided and named (see chapter 1) and, after much debate, settled on the name of Prescott for the new town. McCormick had brought a large number of books with him to set up a town library when they reached their destination. Among these books were the works of the then-esteemed historian William Hickling Prescott, who wrote several volumes of South American history. Though Prescott had died five years earlier and had never set foot in the Southwest, the Arizona officials decided to name the new Arizona capital as an honor to him. The town of Prescott, Arizona, was born.

Arizona's first territorial officials pose for a portrait before departing for the new frontier. *From left to right*: Henry W. Fleury, Joseph P. Allyn, Milton Duffield, Governor John N. Goodwin, Alman Gage and Richard C. McCormick, who would later become Arizona's second governor. *Sharlot Hall Museum.*

A settler named Robert Groom was hired to survey the area, while Governor Goodwin's secretary, Henry W. Fleury, parceled out the first town lots for sale. The prospect of having an actual town to live in drew many of the wildcat miners and settlers from the nearby mountains. Secretary of the Territory Richard C. McCormick started Prescott's first newspaper, the *Arizona Miner*, on March 9, 1864.

Women were scarce, needless to say, but the first marriage in the new territory occurred between John H. Dickson and Mary J. Ehle on November 17, 1864. Governor Goodwin himself performed the ceremony. (While it was recorded as a legal marriage, it could be historically debatable whether the governor had the legal authority to do this, especially when a minister, Hiram W. Reid, had come out with the governor's party and was available.)

The territorial officials were living in tents, and it was decided that the governor certainly needed something better. They contracted with builders John Raible and Daniel Hatz and a few other men to construct a large log structure out of Ponderosa pine trees on the bank of Granite Creek. Construction began in July 1864 and was completed in the fall of that year. At two thousand square feet, it was considered a mansion compared to the tents and cabins the other settlers and citizens were living in. Governor

Goodwin lived on one side of the mansion, while Secretary McCormick lived on the other. Goodwin's secretary, Henry Fleury, reportedly lived with the governor.

In 1865, Richard McCormick took an extended trip to San Francisco, and on his return to the territory, surprised everyone by bringing home a wife, Margaret Griffiths Hunt of Rahway, New Jersey, whom he had met on his trip. After a whirlwind courtship, they traveled to New Jersey to see her family and were married there before returning to Arizona.

As women still were not plentiful in the territory, the young and beautiful Margaret McCormick entranced the citizens of Prescott. She held parties in the Governor's Mansion and became, unofficially, the first lady of Arizona. Sadly, it did not last long. On April 30, 1867, after her husband succeeded Goodwin as governor, she died in childbirth in the mansion at the age of twenty-four. She and the stillborn baby were buried near the mansion, although two years later, her family arranged for her to be exhumed and reburied in her hometown of Rahway, New Jersey.

AMERICAN TERRITORIES WERE EACH allowed to have a delegate seated in the U.S. House of Representatives in Washington, D.C., so an election was held in 1864 to send to the nation's capital the first delegate from Arizona. It was won by Charles Debrille Poston, the man whose lobbying of President Lincoln played a pivotal role in the establishment of the Arizona Territory.

This angered the territorial officials—they already disliked Poston intensely, plus most of them coveted the position of delegate, for it would have allowed them to go home to New England permanently without looking like they were abandoning the territory. The following year, when Poston was up for reelection, he was challenged by Governor John N. Goodwin, who won the election. Goodwin went off to Washington, where he served a single term as territorial delegate, and never returned to Arizona. President Andrew Johnson then appointed Richard McCormick to be the next governor.

Poston did not go quietly and publicly charged that his defeat in the election was due to vote fraud and other political machinations. Seeing an opportunity to finish off the hated Poston, the Arizona Territorial Legislature passed a resolution formally condemning him for his accusations. This ended the political career of Charles D. Poston. He spent the rest of his life holding a few menial jobs, doing some writing and traveling and hoping for a comeback that never materialized. He drew more scorn late in life for converting to the Far Eastern religion of Zoroastrianism, reportedly becoming the first American to do so. He died in poverty in Phoenix on June 24, 1902.

THE CITIZENS OF TUCSON were very angry that their town had not been declared the territorial capital in 1864, as had been expected. They fought back, and only a scant three years later, in 1867, the territorial legislature formally passed a bill moving the capital to Tucson. Governor Richard C. McCormick supported the move. The territorial government packed up and headed to Tucson, with the exception of Henry W. Fleury. Astounded by the move, he stayed behind in Prescott, becoming one of its pioneer citizens. He acquired the title to the Governor's Mansion and lived there until his death in 1895. He went on to become, at various times, probate judge and justice of the peace for Prescott.

Ten years later, in 1877, the capital dispute came up again, resulting in the territorial legislature moving the capital *back* to Prescott. This held until 1889, when territorial governor C. Meyer Zulick and legislator John Robbins speedily pushed a bill through that moved the capital to Phoenix. Many Prescott citizens had gone on record as saying they would react with force to any attempt to move the capital out of Prescott again. Therefore, the legislature passed the bill quietly, Governor Zulick signed it and the officials quickly loaded up everything they needed onto a train and headed out for Los Angeles, where they stayed a couple of days to celebrate and then transferred the shipment onto a train for Phoenix. The people of Prescott didn't know what happened until it was too late. They swore that if Governor Zulick came anywhere near Prescott again, he would be murdered.

So, why did the Arizona Territorial Legislature move the capital around so much? In retrospect, it seems absurd, considering that situations like this never existed in other states or territories. In his later writings, Charles Poston claimed it was a power struggle by different areas of the territory to control who got elected as territorial delegate to the U.S. House of Representatives. (A position Richard McCormick attained after moving the capital to Tucson.) This is as good an explanation as any for the bizarre scenario.

Even after Arizona finally attained statehood in 1912, the capital stayed in Phoenix, where it remains to this day. In Prescott, the 1864 Governor's Mansion still stands; it has had numerous refurbishings over the years, but today it is the centerpiece of Sharlot Hall Museum in Prescott and is the oldest log structure in Arizona still standing on its original site.

IN RECENT YEARS, A curious debate has sprung up about what town should be considered Arizona's first capital. For generations, Prescott was always regarded as the first capital of Arizona, but an argument has lately been advanced that the first capital was Chino Valley, because the governor's party in 1864 had stopped at Fort Whipple at Del Rio Springs and conducted government business there.

The argument favoring Prescott is that only the territorial legislature had the power to declare a capital, and it never convened while the party was at Fort Whipple. On the other hand, the argument favoring Chino Valley/Del Rio Springs is that in the absence of an official declaration the capital was automatically where the governor happened to be—and since the territorial officials conducted business while at Fort Whipple, it is clear they considered it, temporarily at least, the capital.

The debate over which view is valid has become quite spirited in recent times. Older Arizona historians favor the Prescott argument, while younger historians seem to favor Chino Valley. Consequently, while an official verdict is still out, the view that Chino Valley was the first capital has been gaining traction in recent years. In fact, the website for the Chino Valley town government proclaims it as the first capital.

While the present author has his own opinions on this subject, for the purposes of this book, we shall let the readers decide for themselves at this point.

3
Masonic Influence

I t has not been widely examined by historians, but nationwide in the nineteenth century, fraternal organizations and lodges were considered very important. They often carried a great deal of influence in cities and towns, to the point of dictating policy in the communities. America was filled with branches of the Freemasons, Elks, Moose, Oddfellows, Knights of Pythias and other lodges, and membership in one or more lodges was considered a sign of upstanding character. Through most of the nineteenth century, if a man was not a brother in good standing in one or more fraternal organizations, he was not considered to be very respectable.

Certainly, the oldest and best-known of such lodges is Freemasonry and its offshoots. Though its origin is shrouded in mystery, historians can trace the Masonic Lodge to the 1700s, but the lodge itself claims to have existed almost since the beginning of time. The group has, over the centuries, been the target of many conspiracy theories that claim it secretly rules the entire world. Whether claims like that are credible or not, there is no denying Freemasonry has had considerable influence in American history. Most of America's founding fathers were Masons, a fact often ignored by their biographers, but no one denies the presence of certain Masonic symbols on American currency today.

In the new town of Prescott, established as the capital of the new Territory of Arizona, the record indicates that chartering a branch of the Masonic Lodge was an issue of paramount importance to the town and territorial officials and was one of the earliest things they talked about. The first

Masonic meeting to be held in Prescott occurred in 1865 and was held in the Governor's Mansion, with Governor John N. Goodwin himself presiding. The ultimate result was the creation of Aztlan Lodge no. 1, the first Masonic Lodge in Arizona, which exists in Prescott to this day.

On June 23, 1891, at a celebration of the twenty-fifth anniversary of Aztlan Lodge no. 1, Morris Goldwater (who served several terms as mayor of Prescott and was uncle of famed U.S. senator Barry M. Goldwater) delivered a lengthy speech to the lodge summarizing its history. The *Arizona Journal Miner* newspaper printed excerpts from this speech, and it is a fascinating and invaluable historical document, inasmuch as the Masonic Lodge is seldom this open about its past and its inner workings. Some excerpts from Goldwater's speech are as follows:

The first mention I can find of an effort to start a lodge is in a letter written by our lately deceased brother Alexander G. Abell, very worshipful grand secretary of the Grand Lodge of California. It is dated July 29, 1864, and is in reply to a letter written by Brother John Howard, now mayor of our city. In order to insure [sic] *its delivery, it was addressed to Fort Whipple.*

The contents indicate the writer's willingness to do all in his power to help the brethren of Prescott form a lodge. To those who knew Brother Abell, I need not say how much Aztlan Lodge and perhaps every other lodge on the Pacific slope is indebted to him for gratuitous advice and service. For 36 years, he served continuously as secretary of the Grand Lodge of California, and for ability, accuracy, and knowledge of Masonic law and ritual, he was the peer of any member of the craft.

The first recorded minutes of a meeting are without date. It was in the year 1864. The secretary, who was Lieut. Charles Curtis of the U.S. Army, with what was perhaps an excess of zeal, left unwritten many items, which would today be of great value to us. The meeting was held at the house of John N. Goodwin, then governor of the Territory, and is the log building now owned by and the home of Judge H.W. Fleury.

Brother Goodwin presided at the meeting and, after satisfying themselves that all present were masters, it was resolved to apply to the Grand Lodge of California for a dispensation to open a lodge at Prescott. The name selected was Aztlan, and Brother John T. Alsop was chosen as the first master, Brother Joseph Ehle was named as senior warden, and Brother H. Brooks as junior warden. This petition was signed by nine master Masons. Of the signers, some we know are dead. Brothers Brooks and Ehle are still with us, and of the others all traces are lost. It being necessary to have a recommendation from the nearest lodge, Brother Joseph Lennon was selected to carry the petition to Santa Fe and procure from the lodge there the proper endorsement. At the next meeting, which likewise has no date on the records, the sum of three hundred dollars was subscribed with which to furnish a hall. The place chosen was not named, but Brothers Brooks and Ehle inform us it was in an attic over what is now known as Fitz Jason's Saloon, and then as now owned by Mr. Levi Bashford.

On the return of Brother Lennon from Santa Fe with the necessary recommendation, Brother John N. Goodwin was chosen to present the petition to the grand master of California. Brother Goodwin presented the petition on April 23, 1865, and the dispensation prayed for was granted. Owing to the inability of Brother Ehle to procure a demit [resignation] *from his lodge, Brother Brooks was named senior warden and Brother Herbert Bowers was chosen as junior.*

In one of Brother Abell's letters written at this time, I note as indicative of the hardships of the day the following sentence, "As the war is now over, there will be no difficulty in your members communicating with their several mother lodges and procuring their demits."

The lodge, on the 23rd of July 1865, was duly opened, and begun work. On Oct. 12, 1865, the M.W. Grand Lodge was pleased to continue the dispensation in force until the annual meeting of 1866.

The regular meeting night was set for the last Saturday night of each month and has so remained until the present time, and it is pleasing to note that the lodge during its 25 years of life has never failed to hold its monthly session.

On September 30th, 1865, the first work was done by the new Lodge. The Degree of Entered Apprentice was conferred in Bro. A.O. Noyes and J.G. Mitchell, and Bro. Barr was raised to the degree of Master Mason.

On January 2nd, 1866, we find the first record of a lodge funeral. The deceased Brother being Stephen Lee, of Eugene City, Oregon. In the files of the Arizona Miner *of 1864, owned by Mr. B.H. Weaver, there is a notice of a Masonic funeral, although there was at that time no lodge.* [Here Goldwater errs, as all other sources show that the *Arizona Miner* newspaper was owned by territorial secretary Richard C. McCormick in 1864.]

On January 27th, 1866, we find another indication of the results of the war in a resolution requiring all dues and fees to be paid the lodge in gold or silver coin, or in gold dust.

Exterior of the Masonic Temple on Cortez Street is seen in this undated photo. Constructed in 1907, Aztlan Lodge no. 1 met here until 1982. The building still stands. *Sharlot Hall Museum.*

In March 1866, a Building Committee was appointed to secure a lot with a view to building a hall, but the matter was indefinitely postponed. And it may as well be stated here that similar committees have been several times appointed and the resulting action has invariably been the same.

In August 1866, the last meeting under the dispensation was held. The debts of the Lodge were all paid, the books, papers, and dispensations were forwarded to California by Lt. Barr for examination, and the Grand Lodge was by a vote asked to change the name of the lodge from Aztlan to Arizona. Five months elapsed and in January 1867, the glad tidings came that the charter had arrived.

No reason is assigned for the refusal of the Grand Lodge to change the name, but the charter had been granted under the name and number of Aztlan Lodge No. 177. This charter, which now adorns our Lodge Room, was brought from San Francisco to La Paz by Mr. Charles B. Genung and from La Paz to Prescott by Bro. Joseph R. Walker. [This is legendary explorer Joseph Rutherford Walker] *It arrived here January 21st, 1867, and notices were immediately printed and distributed around Prescott and its vicinity for a meeting to be held January 26th. The Brethren assembled and Past Master John Martin duly constituted the Lodge and installed its officers.*

In May 1867, a Committee was appointed to raise and re-inter the body of Bro. William P. Jones, who had been killed by Indians near Prescott in June 1864. The Committee selected as a suitable place the present cemetery, and reported to the Lodge that Governor R.C. (Richard) McCormick had generously donated the ground for a Masonic cemetery, and appropriate resolutions of thanks were passed and ordered sent to him.

I shall not attempt to give you the details of the work done by the lodge in this early period of its history. The minutes show much labor performed. The Lodge by its standing proves whether this work was square and true. There are records of the deaths of many brethren inhumanly butchered by the ruthless savage, with no friend near to cheer them in the hour of death or bear a last affectionate remembrance to the loved ones left to mourn their fate. Kind and loving hands brought and laid their remains to rest, and the Lodge was the first to convey the sad tidings to sorrowing relatives. In November 1867, the Lodge asked for a reduction of rent and the price was fixed at $22 a month, gold coin. In May 1868, permission was given the IOOF to hold informal meetings in the hall, and $150 were expended for jewels and regalia.

In October 1868, a new Lodge Room was chosen in the second story on the Southwest corner of Montezuma and Gurley streets, over the Diana Saloon, and where the Hotel Burke now stands. $466 were spent in furnishing the hall, and $320 was paid for freight on the furniture and carpets brought from California. In this month, the fence around the cemetery was built. The cost was defrayed by public subscription, and there

This undated photo shows the interior of the main meeting hall in the Masonic Temple on Cortez Street. Owing to the secrecy of the order, Masonic interior photos are rare. *Sharlot Hall Museum.*

is no record of the amount, but the lowest bid for painting the fence was $650, while for whitewashing it only $350 were asked.

In December 1869, the first public installation took place. It was held in the old Courthouse, Past Master Col. E.D. Baker acting as Installing Officer, and Bro. John A. Rush delivering an oration.

Morris Goldwater's published speech is a remarkable historical document, inasmuch as it was, and still is, very rare for the Freemasons to publicly talk about the inner workings of the lodge like this, to say nothing of the revelation that many of Prescott's most prominent men from its earliest days were Masons. Goldwater remained an active member of the lodge until his death in 1939.

Eventually, Prescott Aztlan Lodge did find a home. In 1907, they purchased a large plot of land on North Cortez Street to build a large Masonic Temple. The cornerstone was ceremonially laid with much public fanfare on October

19, 1907, with oratory speeches by prominent lodge members Judge Edmund W. Wells and attorney LeRoy Anderson. Ultimately, a beautiful three-story edifice was constructed, which remained the home of the lodge for decades.

However, this was destined not to be permanent either. The lodge sold the building around 1982, for reasons not entirely clear at this writing. Perhaps continued upkeep of the aging building was getting too costly, or perhaps declining membership made a smaller facility desirable—or perhaps a combination of reasons. But the building still stands, used by offices and storefronts today. Aztlan Lodge currently meets in its own building on Willow Creek Road, which it shares with a bank.

4

IN OLD CHINATOWN

Although not often discussed anymore, the Arizona Territory had a rather large population of Chinese immigrants. They started arriving already in the late 1860s, only a few years after the establishment of the territory, and before long, virtually all sizable towns in Arizona had somewhat segregated "Chinatowns," including Tucson, Kingman and Prescott.

Historians still have differing opinions on what brought the Chinese to Arizona, but the most logical explanation is that they came from California. That state had an extremely high population of Chinese immigrants, and many poorer Chinese men had gotten jobs as the manual laborers who built the railroads across that state, where they were referred to disparagingly as "coolies." California also had small numbers of Chinese placer miners in remote areas.

When the railroads were finished and the placer mining played out, many Chinese returned to the big cities of California, such as San Francisco and Los Angeles. Others, on hearing of new territory opening in Arizona, started to migrate there. Most (though admittedly not all) Chinese immigrants in the West were men, having left their wives and families in China while they came to America with the hope of earning money and sending it back home. By 1868, reportedly, twenty Chinese men were working at the Vulture Mine near the town of Wickenburg in Arizona.

The first Chinese man to arrive in Prescott came in the early summer of 1869. Naturally, he stood out, and the *Arizona Miner* newspaper reported on May 29, 1869, "We have heretofore neglected to inform our readers that a veritable young Celestial arrived at Fort Whipple a short time ago. Should he live long enough to become a man, Yavapai county will contain one Chinaman."

The *Arizona Miner* was now owned by journalist John Marion, who had purchased the newspaper from Governor Richard C. McCormick when McCormick and the territorial capital moved to Tucson in 1867. Marion was typical of his era in terms of racial attitudes toward the Chinese or any other minority race. The *Miner*'s ongoing coverage of Chinese immigration was condescending and insulting, using epithets like "Celestial" and "Mongolian" to describe them. On November 27, 1869, the *Miner* reported, "Three more Chinamen arrived here during the week and have gone to work. There are now four of them in this vicinity, which is quite enough."

The following week, the *Miner* noted on December 4, 1869, "Since our last, some ten or twelve more Chinamen have arrived."

And so, the influx of Chinese immigrants into Prescott continued. Many of the men found work locally doing manual labor, while others tried their hands at placer mining, as they had done in California. Despite Prescott's infancy as a town, Granite Street was already developing a reputation as the "lower end" of the community, with a less-than-stellar reputation. Consequently, rent was cheap there, and as the Chinese community earned money, Granite Street was a neighborhood where they could afford to live. It would become Chinatown for its duration.

As Chinese men continued to arrive, Prescott's white residents started to become alarmed. A small rival newspaper, the *Prescott Enterprise*, asserted on October 10, 1877: "Still they come! Two more Celestials arrived in Prescott on the stage last Sunday morning. The Chinese population of Prescott is getting to be pretty numerous, and unless something is done to stop this immigration, they soon will overrun everything."

Meanwhile, the *Arizona Miner* reported on October 3, 1879, "Prescott has about 75 or 80 Chinamen, which is 75 or 80 too many. Now is a good time to get rid of them."

But these press incitements to violence did not have the desired effect, and by the time the 1880s came, Chinatown on Granite Street was an established part of Prescott, albeit a downtrodden, disrespected one. Living in their ramshackle cabins in the neighborhood, the Chinese residents began opening their own businesses on Granite Street, including laundries and restaurants, to serve not only their own people but also any white people who might want to patronize them. For all their hostility toward the Chinese, Prescott residents were not above using their businesses if

The Chinese joss house on Granite Street in the 1880s. It was used as a community center and house of spiritual worship by Prescott's Chinese immigrants. *Sharlot Hall Museum.*

it meant saving a few dollars. Even among white residents, men greatly outnumbered women in Prescott at this time, and single men did not relish doing their own laundry.

Meanwhile, on Montezuma Street (only one block north of Granite Street), a change was occurring. A string of wild saloons and low-grade eating joints was springing up to serve the local miners, ranchers and cowboys who wanted a good stiff drink (or more) after a hard day of work. This area soon developed the moniker of "Whiskey Row," a name it retains to this day. The Chinese men of Prescott were in luck with the formation of Whiskey Row, as they were able to get jobs as cooks and bartenders there. The business owners knew that the Chinese would work for less money than white labor would.

At some point during this period, the Chinese men added a second story to one of their buildings on Granite Street near the intersection with Goodwin

Street. This became the community's joss house, or rather, the Chinese temple where they worshipped their gods and held community meetings. The interior likely contained small statues and images (called "josses") of the Chinese gods, which they could kneel to and worship. Photos of the exterior of the joss house have survived, but not of the interior.

ALMOST ALL OF THESE Chinese immigrants were men. They were either single or had left wives in China while they came to America to seek their fortunes. Naturally, women and sexual comforts were greatly missed by these men. This led to a booming trade of slave and sex trafficking between Chinese human traffickers in China and the Pacific coast of the United States. Women were often kidnapped in China and shipped to San Francisco or some other Pacific coast town, where they would be rented or sold into prostitution in the various Chinatowns in the western United States.

On March 11, 1874, the *Arizona Miner* reported the arrival of Prescott's first Chinese woman: "Wickenburg stage arrived at about half past six, Thursday evening, with several passengers, and seven packs of mail. Among the passengers was a Chinese female, the first that has ever visited this town, and section of country, and, we hope, the last."

An 1878 portrait of an unidentified Chinese woman in Prescott. Since Chinese women were scarce even on Granite Street, she was likely a prostitute or a sex trafficking victim *Sharlot Hall Museum.*

She was possibly a prostitute or sex trafficking victim sent to service the Chinese men of Prescott. More would follow, as the 1880 census indicates five Chinese prostitutes on Granite Street.

Prostitution was legal in most of America at this time, and as Prescott grew, so did the demand for such services among the working men of Prescott. The northern section of Granite Street became the red-light district, with its brothels and cribs. With prostitutes on one end and Chinatown on the other, both overlapping, Granite Street solidified its reputation as Prescott's skid row area.

Chinese immigrants in the Southwest were largely itinerant. Peasants and manual laborers, they spoke very little English. Most could not speak the language at all, and those who could had only picked up a few words and phrases while working on the railroads. When they settled in areas like Granite Street in Prescott, they opened their businesses and ran them the way they might have done in China—the only way they knew how. This low-key type of management did not have much effect in America.

But as the years passed, it was inevitable that some Chinese merchants would start getting the hang of the American way of doing things. In Prescott, Granite Street laundryman George Ah Fat became the first Chinese businessman to buy a paid ad in the *Arizona Miner* for his establishment on September 2, 1871. The verbiage of the ad was flowery enough that it was likely written by someone else at the laundryman's request. His name was almost certainly not George, but he also recognized that having an anglicized name would help him in a white man's town. The advertising must have had the desired effect, for George Ah Fat stayed in business. He would become Prescott's first Chinese entrepreneur.

On February 20, 1874, the *Miner* reported disparagingly on an affray in Chinatown in which George Ah Fat had physically threatened a rival laundryman on Granite Street. Though specific details are lacking, the incident apparently caused a new round of anti-Chinese sentiment to flare up among Prescott's white people, for the following week, the *Miner* ran a letter signed by six Chinese men, asserting that they wanted to get along with Prescott's townspeople and placing the blame for problems in Chinatown with George Ah Fat and his employees at his laundry.

George was becoming well known enough in Prescott that the *Miner* started to occasionally report on his comings and goings, as newspapers of that era often did for prominent citizens. The April 9, 1875 edition reported that George Ah Fat had returned from a trip and brought back to Prescott with him his brother from China.

So-called bad neighborhoods, then as now, always seem to have some kind of trouble going on. In March 1877, a Chinese man named Sam Lee was arrested at George Ah Fat's request for allegedly attempting to blow up George's laundry with a can of blasting powder. It is not known how the case turned out.

On September 6, 1878, the *Miner* reported on George Ah Fat's return to Prescott from an eight-month trip to China. The newspaper disparagingly

Unidentified Chinese man sits for a portrait at Prescott's Erwin Baer photography studio in Prescott, circa 1870s or 1880s. *Sharlot Hall Museum.*

scoffed that he had probably made the trip to dispose of the "spoils" from his business.

But George was perhaps the first really successful Chinese businessman in Prescott. He had made enough money that he decided it was time to branch out, and he opened two new businesses in 1880. One was what could be termed a curio shop, called Jow Hop & Co. The paid ads he bought in the *Miner* promised both Japanese and Chinese goods, including silk handkerchiefs, collars and "the best teas." The ads state that this store was located "next door to Jackson's stand" on Montezuma Street. George Ah Fat had expanded one block up from Granite Street to Montezuma and was perhaps the first Chinese immigrant in Prescott to actually own a business in a white section of town.

Simultaneously, he leased a restaurant on Whiskey Row from owner D.C. Thorne, called the Cabinet Chop House (likely part of Thorne's prominent Cabinet Saloon). In his paid ads, George promised first-class service and "ice cream every day."

George Ah Fat had bucked impossible odds and found some measure of acceptance as a businessman among Prescott's white population. But it seems he overestimated that acceptance. To further broaden his business, George announced that he was turning part of the Cabinet Chop House building into a boardinghouse at eight dollars per week for renters. Now, in that era, no white people would ever rent from a Chinese landlord, so it must be presumed that his tenants were other Chinese men moving up from Granite Street. Clearly, this did not sit well with the Prescott townspeople, and there must have been some repercussions, for on July 16, 1880, George Ah Fat asked the *Miner* to report that he was no longer taking in boarders at the Cabinet Chop House.

But the damage must have been done. The last documented references to George Ah Fat in Prescott are from 1881. After that, he seems to drop off the face of recorded history. He must have left town, and his eventual fate is unknown at this time.

An interesting sidebar to the story of George Ah Fat pertains to Sam Lee, who George had accused in 1877 of trying to blow up his laundry. Later that year, in August, Sam Lee got into a fight with another Chinese man whose name was variously reported in the newspapers as Ah Fork or Jim Ah Fawk. The altercation occurred just out of town along Lynx Creek, when Sam Lee pulled a knife and stabbed Ah Fork. At that point, Ah Fork was able to pull his own knife and stabbed Sam Lee to death.

Shortly afterward, a coroner's inquest jury, led by county coroner Dr. Warren E. Day, ruled the homicide to have been self-defense, but later on, Ah Fork was arrested for it anyway.

NATIONWIDE, NEWSPAPERS OF THIS period often regaled their readers with news of crime committed by minority races, including Chinese. Reading these old reports today, one gets the impression that racial minorities committed the vast majority of crimes in towns like Prescott, though this was not the case. Most of these reported crimes were petty, often involving minor assaults or thefts among themselves. The press gleefully played these up while ignoring similar petty crimes committed by white people. Most such cases ended up being brought before the local justice of the peace instead of superior court.

There is one such case from Prescott that stands out today, simply because of who was involved. On or about October 1, 1879, John H. Behan went to a Chinese laundry on Granite Street for unknown reasons. An argument of some kind broke out, resulting in about half a dozen Chinese men attacking Behan with clubs, severely injuring him. The men were later arrested.

Behan had held a number of official positions in Yavapai County over the years, including sheriff. But within a couple of years after this incident, he left Prescott for Tombstone and Cochise County, where he will forever be remembered as an enemy of Wyatt Earp.

BY THE 1880s, THE Chinese community on Granite Street had become pretty well established in Prescott, and the other townspeople, though not really accepting of them, at least tolerated their presence in the community. There were still some problems—Chinese immigrants across America had brought vices of gambling and opium smoking with them. In most places, gambling was legal, but opium was another matter. Chinese gambling houses and opium dens had a fairly steady supply of business among lower-class white men, and Prescott was no different.

An 1879 edition of the *Arizona Miner* noted, "The Chinese dens of Prescott carry on quite an extensive business in the way of opium smoking. There are several persons, not altogether Chinese in nationality, who pay for the privilege of inhaling the intoxicating fumes from opium pipes in the celestial dens of Prescott."

But in 1880, Prescott decided to take action against opium use and passed an ordinance prohibiting its use or sale within the town limits. On a national level, the U.S. Congress in 1887 passed a law prohibiting opium use in America, except for medical purposes. Chinese immigrants argued that opium was part of their culture, but white authorities were having none of it.

Consequently, many arrests for opium use or underground sales of it started to skyrocket. Prescott was no different, as smaller lawmen—usually deputies or constables—regularly raided Chinatown on Granite Street to make arrests for opium violations. The *Prescott Courier* newspaper of February 17, 1893, reported on such a raid, this one conducted by Prescott constable Louis C. Miller:

> *Night before last Constable Miller, with the aid of two citizens, raided a Chinese opium joint of middle Granite street, capturing twelve opium smokers, four pipes, and several cases of opium. There were three whites and nine Chinamen captured. Thirteen persons were in the room at the time of the raid, but one got away. The constable stated that when the room was entered the fiends were all lying in bunks arranged around the walls one above another, and each prisoner was in a stupefied state until they had walked a short distance in the open air. They were brought before Judge Noyes, who held them in $50 bail each, trial to take place before him at 10 o'clock tomorrow. A white man and woman gave the bail and were released. The other ten prisoners went to jail.*

Gambling was another matter. Gambling was almost universally legal at this time, and the saloons on Whiskey Row kept up a brisk business with Prescott's miners and cowboys. The Chinese were inveterate gamblers, but they were not particularly welcome in the white man's saloons, so they opened their own dens in the back rooms of Granite Street. The July 25, 1879 edition of the *Arizona Miner* reported, "The most consummate gamblers to be found anywhere are among the Chinese of Prescott. Several Chinese games are running every night in this town, and we have not heard of their paying a gambling license."

And so it was.

ANOTHER ASPECT OF THEIR culture that Chinese immigrants brought to America was their secret societies, popularly known as Tongs. The Tongs were something of an underground government for the Chinese, representing the interests of their members, often through violent means. Tong agents and their "hatchet men" (assassins) were swift and clever enough that American authorities were often unable to apprehend them when crimes were committed.

Reportedly, the first Tong in America was the Chee Kung Tong, established in San Francisco. They also became known in America as the Chinese Masons, even though they had no relationship to Freemasonry. The Chee Kung Tong swiftly spread throughout all Chinese immigrant communities in the United States, including Prescott. As with any large group, dissenting factions broke away and formed their own branches, or Tongs. The result was the bloody Tong wars that besieged Chinese neighborhoods in West Coast cities in the late nineteenth and early twentieth centuries.

By 1909, the Chee Kung Tong (or Chinese Masons) had become open enough that members started talking to the white newspapers. That year, a top official of the Tong, Lem You, was making a tour of the Chinese communities in America, and he came to Prescott with the Tong's secretary, Jo Get Chin. The *Prescott Journal Miner* newspaper on April 14, 1909, reported a statement by him. In it, Lem denied there were any Tong wars going on in California and asserted that 80 percent of Prescott's Chinese population on Granite Street were members of the Chee Kung Tong. After staying in Prescott for two days, Lem left for Tucson.

Perhaps the worst recorded flare-up of Tong violence in early Arizona began in neighboring Mohave County in 1926, but it would touch Prescott. On October 20, 1926, Tom King (his given name was Gen Quen Yeck), a restaurateur in the town of Kingman, was peeling potatoes in his American Kitchen restaurant when five Asian men with guns burst through the door and opened fire, killing King instantly.

Mohave County authorities hit the trail of the murderers and caught up with them at the California state line. The five men were identified as B.W.L. Sam, Shew Chin, Jew Har, Gee King Long and Wong Lung. All five were further identified as hatchet men for the Bing Kong Tong. The dead man, Tom King, was revealed to have been a longstanding member of the Hop Sing Tong. Both Tongs had been warring in America's larger cities for years, and now the violence had spread off the beaten path to Arizona. The Hop Sing Tong was regarded as one of the most powerful in America by the 1920s, perhaps second only to the Chee Kung Tong itself.

Alarmed by the outbreak of Tong activity in Mohave County, Sheriff William Mahoney ordered a general "shakedown" of all Chinese residents, confiscating guns and ordering several of them to leave town. (These were the days when lawmen could legally do things like this.) Mahoney also asked Yavapai County to take the five Tong killers to jail in Prescott, ostensibly as a safeguard against attempts on their lives by other Tong hatchet men. The five were lodged in the Prescott jail shortly after that.

In December 1926, the Tong killers went on trial in Prescott. Marring the proceedings was the sudden and mysterious disappearance of Don On, a restaurant customer who had been the only eyewitness to Tom King's murder. He was never found, dead or alive, and it was presumed that he met with foul play at the hands of the Bing Kong Tong.

Despite this setback, the jury found the five Tong hatchet men guilty of first-degree murder, and they were sentenced to hang at the Arizona State Prison in Florence. Their lawyers, undoubtedly paid for by the Bing Kong Tong, immediately appealed to the Arizona State Supreme Court. This delayed the executions for some time. The possibility of a successful appeal alarmed the Hop Sing Tong, which dispatched its top attorney, J.N. Young, to Arizona from Chicago.

Arriving in Prescott on March 22, 1927, attorney Young immediately employed several prominent local attorneys (including Mohave County Superior Court judge E. Elmo Bollinger, Yavapai County attorney W.E. Paterson and assistant Yavapai County attorney John J. Sweeney) to represent the Hop Sing Tong during the appeals process. Attorney Young told the *Prescott Courier* newspaper that the Hop Sing Tong had over $1 million to spend to ensure that the killers' appeals would not be successful. Young also told the *Courier* that there were twenty Chinese businessmen in Prescott who were members of the Hop Sing Tong, a revelation that surely caused discomfort among Prescott's white residents.

The Arizona State Supreme Court upheld the death sentences of the five Tong killers, but their execution was postponed again when Frank Craig, another witness at the trial, recanted his testimony and claimed that he had been bribed by attorney J.N. Young. After much legal wrangling and debating among the courts and the State Board of Pardons and Paroles, the execution date was set again, this time for June 23, 1928. At the last minute, Wong Lung's death sentence was commuted to life in prison because of his age; the Tong hatchet man was only seventeen years old.

On June 23, 1928, the four assassins—B.W.L. Sam, Shew Chin, Jew Har and Gee King Long—were hanged at the Arizona State Prison in Florence, one right after the other. A legal quadruple hanging was rare even in those days, and in retrospect, it is surprising that the Tong murder case has been largely forgotten. Perhaps this is due to latter-day racial sensitivities and the fact that the story still has a chill to it, despite the passage of almost one hundred years.

Do Chinese Tongs still exist? Historians of Chinese culture are in debate about this. The Chee Kung Tong does, in fact, survive, but some of its branches have formally adopted their old alias, Chinese Masons. Today, they claim to be a peaceful group working to protect Chinese interests in various nations. At the same time, there have been news reports from California in recent years reporting that members of the Tong have been arrested on racketeering charges.

Through the 1880s, life continued as usual in Prescott and for Prescott's Chinese on Granite Street. There were no white-owned laundries in Prescott at the time, forcing white people to patronize the Chinese laundries if they did not wish to wash their own clothes. Men addicted to vices like opium found their needs easily met in the Chinese dens. And white merchants in Prescott had discovered that the Chinese were willing to work for less money than white labor, so they hired the Asians to work as cooks and waiters and similar jobs in their establishments. But anti-Chinese sentiment did crop up from time to time.

Stephen Giberton Marcou was a French expatriate who moved to Prescott from Tucson in the early 1880s. He seemed to be a jack of all trades—he opened a law office in Prescott and offered language tutorial services in both French and Spanish, as he spoke both fluently in addition to English. Marcou sometimes found work as a court interpreter when any Mexicans were brought to trial, and there are records from the Yavapai County Board of Supervisors that it occasionally paid him for burials. As Marcou was not a mortician, it can only be deduced that he earned extra money as a gravedigger for the county when it needed to bury indigents at the potter's field at Citizens Cemetery.

On top of all that, Stephen Marcou was a horticulturalist, and he opened a nursery called Prescott Garden, where he sold plants, trees and shrubs to those wishing to landscape their property with such things. One of his ads for Prescott Garden notes, "No dogs or Chinese allowed on the grounds."

Indeed, like many, Marcou was disgusted with Chinese immigration throughout the Southwest, and by 1886, he decided to do something about it. He began writing a series of editorials for Prescott's newspapers, calling for the formation in town of an Anti-Chinese League. Such leagues had been formed with varying degrees of success in other Southwest towns that had seen a heavy influx of Chinese immigrants; Marcou decided Prescott was ripe for one to drive the Asians completely out of the village.

In his opening screed published in the *Arizona Miner* of March 21, 1886, Marcou wrote:

That a majority of the citizens of Yavapai do not want to encourage the immigration into the county of the Chinese who are being expelled from the Pacific coast is a fact so obvious that no arguments are needed to demonstrate it; but the best way to get rid of the heathens is the problem which should engage our attention.

The first thing to be done is to organize an anti-Chinese League, composed of respectable citizens, every member of which shall pledge himself to obey the lawful mandates of a duly elected Executive Board; this will insure united and harmonious action without which little good can be affected.

Some of the measures which will probably be discussed by the Board and adopted, if after due consideration, they are deemed likely to advance the interests of the League, may be the following:

All members to patronize exclusively restaurants, boarding houses, and hotels where no Chinese cooks or waiters are employed.

All members to abstain from voting for any office seekers who employ or deal with Chinese or are known to sympathize with them.

The creation of a fund by small monthly contributions from each member of the League, to be used for encouraging the establishment of white laundries and other industries monopolized by the Mongols.

The Chinese have not yet gained such a foothold in our community as in some of the counties of the Pacific coast, and it is reasonable to expect that they can be got rid of with less trouble and by using less energetic means than have had to be used there.

The best time to abate a nuisance is when it is in its incipient stage and the Chinese are a nuisance in Yavapai.

In subsequent missives in the newspapers, Marcou alleged that the Chinese were injurious to the economies of Prescott and Yavapai County.

He contended that they were taking jobs away from white people, that Chinese businesses were taking customers from white-owned establishments and, more importantly, that the money was not staying local. Marcou contended, probably correctly, that the Chinese were sending the money they were making to their families in China. "It is, I think, no exaggeration to say that more than $100,000 of our money has found its way to China," Marcou thundered on March 31, 1886, "since the unlucky day that the first Chinaman was allowed to establish himself in our county." It was an eerie foreshadowing of a very similar argument used today against immigration from Mexico and Central and South America.

Marcou left a petition at Aitken's Cigar Store for residents to sign who wanted the Chinese to be driven out of Prescott. In another manifesto in the *Arizona Miner*, he sent out a call that probably went over like a lead balloon among the women of Prescott: "Now, God helps those who help themselves. Let every woman who is desirous and able to do housework and take in washing at reasonable rates, make the fact known, either by advertising in the daily papers or by leaving her name at Aitken's Store."

But after acquiring over one hundred signatures on his petitions, Stephen Marcou called a meeting, and an Anti-Chinese League was officially formed in Prescott. Prescott newspaperman John H. Marion, who had penned the first negative coverage of the Chinese in 1869, was elected president of the league, though he resigned soon afterward for unknown reasons and was replaced by former Prescott mayor I.P. Ingwersen. Other prominent members of the league included George H. Schuerman and Patrick Ford, a Civil War hero who had retired to Prescott and held a variety of positions in the community.

The Anti-Chinese League held monthly meetings in the parlor of the Pioneer Hotel. But unlike similar leagues in other towns, they had agreed to methods of boycott instead of vigilante violence. Consequently, the League had no teeth. A number of businesses, including the *Prescott Courier* newspaper, started advertising that they hired only white people as their employees. But without the specter of violence overhead, the Granite Street Chinese held their ground, and few left Prescott as a result.

In the end, Prescott's Anti-Chinese League ran out of steam after only about a year. This might be partly due to their methods not having the desired results and partly due to the unexpected death of their founder, Stephen G. Marcou, who passed away on September 2, 1887, of "chronic dysentery" at the Fort Whipple hospital. He was forty-five years old, and his death occurred only a few weeks after he was convicted of assault and battery of his wife, Rose. (He was fined twenty dollars plus court costs by Justice of the Peace Henry W. Fleury.) In addition to his widow, he left behind a three-year-old daughter.

As Marcou was a Freemason and a member of Aztlan Lodge no. 1 in Prescott, he was buried in the Masonic Cemetery in town. His wife, Rose Marcou, continued to live in Prescott until her death in 1920.

WITH THE FAILURE OF the Anti-Chinese League, as well as the passage of time, it was inevitable that another Chinese entrepreneur (as George Ah Fat had been) would rise from the ranks in Prescott. His name was Joe Ah Jew.

Joe had first attracted attention in 1884, when he became the first and only Chinese naturalized U.S. citizen in the Arizona Territory. The judge who granted him U.S. citizenship did so in defiance of the Exclusion Act of 1882, which barred Chinese people from becoming U.S. citizens. Because of this, a historical argument could be made that Joe's citizenship was invalid, but nevertheless, it was granted to him.

To obtain U.S. citizenship through naturalization, Joe Ah Jew had to be in America for at least five years, as that was the customary waiting period after filing. Joe also apparently had learned to speak, read and write English, which was another requirement for naturalization. Unlike most Chinese immigrants of the era, Joe also tried to fit in by dressing in Western attire, as evidenced by the only known surviving photograph of him.

Restauranteur Joe Ah Jew, who was Arizona's first Chinese naturalized U.S. citizen. He defied difficult odds in the nineteenth century by earning some measure of respect in Prescott's white community. *Sharlot Hall Museum.*

The year 1885 found Joe Ah Jew in the town of Ash Fork, about fifty miles from Prescott, operating a restaurant. However, on April 25, 1885, he was burned out when a fire destroyed two-thirds of the town.

The year 1886 found him working as a cook in the Reception Restaurant in Prescott, but as a proud U.S. citizen, Joe was dissatisfied being restricted largely to Granite Street. Eventually, he purchased Ben Butler's Chop House, a restaurant next to the Cob Web

Saloon on Whiskey Row, becoming only the second Chinese man (after George Ah Fat) to operate a business in the white section of town.

Ben Butler's name stayed on the chop house, Joe clearly recognizing the business value of an "American" name on his business. Ads for Ben Butler's Chop House, listing Joe Ah Jew as proprietor, ran in Prescott's newspapers from 1889 to 1891. The restaurant was open twenty-four hours a day (unusual for a restaurant in that era), and Joe's ads promised "Fresh oysters and game in season."

Apparently, Joe sold the chop house to another Granite Street resident in 1891, as later ads listed the proprietors as "Fong Murphy and Co." After that, Joe's fortunes seem to have declined somewhat. An ad in the November 27, 1895 edition of the *Arizona Journal Miner* lists him as a partner in a small Granite Street shop that sold silk shirts, handkerchiefs, rugs, tea sets, et cetera. After that, little is known of him. A brief article in the September 6, 1919 *Arizona Journal Miner* notes that he would be leaving Prescott to return to China permanently. Somewhere along the way, he had apparently purchased an establishment called the Winsor Restaurant, as this article notes he had sold it to another Chinese man before his departure. Full details are lacking.

THE GRUDGING ACCEPTANCE OF the Chinese in Prescott led to discussions that it might be wise to try to "Americanize" them. The U.S. government had already instituted such programs by force on Native Americans, forcing their children to attend Indian Schools to try to teach them the ways of the white man. But since the Chinese were not government prisoners as the Native Americans were, proponents of Americanizing the Chinese knew their programs would have to be voluntary. They would have to persuade the immigrants that leaving their culture for the American way would be to their benefit.

Stepping up to the plate was the First Congregational Church of Prescott, along with one of its associate pastors, Theodore W. Otis. Otis had arrived in Prescott in the 1870s, opened a store and held a variety of positions in town at one time or another, including postmaster and district court judge. Otis had been one of the few white people in town to actually befriend the Chinese, and he and his wife had in fact adopted a Chinese child along the way, June Moy. Accounts differ on how this came about—some have stated the young girl had run away from a brutal foster father on Granite Street and sought shelter with the Otises and that she had most likely been shipped

Group photo of Pastor Theodore W. Otis's Chinese Sunday school class at the First Congregational Church in Prescott, circa 1895. *Sharlot Hall Museum.*

to Granite Street by Pacific coast Chinese sex traffickers. Other accounts are kinder, stating that Mr. and Mrs. Otis adopted the child with the consent of the foster father.

With his relationship with the Chinese, Theodore W. Otis seemed the ideal choice to teach the First Congregational Church's Chinese Sunday School class, where students would be taught to speak English, learn other Western ways and be converted to Christianity. The Sunday School opened in March 1895 with ten students who had answered the call from Granite Street, realizing that it would be advantageous to them to learn these things. Within a year, the class had grown to thirty-five Chinese students.

In February 1896, Pastor Otis decided it was time to show Prescott the success of the Chinese Sunday School class. He organized a variety show entertainment to be performed by his students in the Congregational Church itself. A large crowd of Prescott's white citizens attended, many undoubtedly drawn by curiosity, to see if the Chinese could really become what they considered "civilized."

Reporting on the event, the *Arizona Journal Miner* stated that two hymns, "There Is a Happy Land" and "Stand Up for Jesus," translated into Chinese, were sung by the students. This was followed by a student named Lou Slung

June Moy, the Chinese adopted child of Theodore W. Otis. Although Otis was a prominent citizen in Prescott, details about the girl are elusive today. *Sharlot Hall Museum.*

reading a New Testament passage in both English and Chinese. Then, Charley Wan (see following section) told an old Chinese fable in English, and student Kim Sam played music on a Chinese harp. Closing out the performance were students Chen Chung, Lou Dick and Quen Long Hing playing music together on a fiddle, a banjo and a flute.

It is unclear how many years Deacon Otis's Chinese Sunday School lasted—it seems that it didn't last for very many years. Today, of course, history has roundly condemned all efforts of the era to Americanize ethnic minorities. But at the time, such efforts were viewed by well-meaning white people as beneficial charity, an effort to help immigrants assimilate into a largely Anglo English-speaking country. The success of such programs was mixed, and the efforts eventually died out with changing times.

CHARLEY WAN WAS ANOTHER Chinese immigrant who tried to assimilate into American society. His real name was Jan Con Sang, but as with George Ah Fat and others, he saw advantages to sporting an Anglicized name while in this country.

Jan is believed to have first arrived in the Southwest circa 1874, and he worked a variety of jobs, including in restaurants. The first record of him in Prescott occurs in 1882, when he placed a series of ads in the *Arizona Miner* for his business (under his American name Charley Wan), the Prescott Dining Rooms, which was actually a boardinghouse, presumably on Granite Street. His rates were eight dollars per week.

Unlike many of Prescott's Chinese, Jan managed to make a few friends among the white citizens of Prescott. His youth and enthusiasm seem to have put him over. He joined Theodore W. Otis's Chinese Sunday School class at the First Congregational Church in 1895 and became a staple of that denomination. In April 1896, the church sent a delegation to a meeting of the church's association in Tempe, and Charley Wan went with them and read a paper pertaining to the Chinese converts. It is also known that he had made friends with local prominent citizens like Moses Hazeltine and Edwin C. Payne.

Both of Prescott's newspapers reported in July 1896 that Charley had been proselytizing on the street in front of the Hotel Burke and that he was soon departing for San Francisco to undergo training to become a Christian missionary in his native China. Although it is unclear exactly when, Jan Con Sang aka Charley Wan did indeed return to China.

Back in his native land, Jan Con Sang entered into a partnership to establish a large mercantile store, the Sincere Company Ltd., which grew to be quite successful, and it opened branches across China in its major cities. This made Jan a wealthy man, but he did not forget his friends in Prescott. He visited at least once and wrote letters (in English, which he had learned to write) to his old friend Moses Hazeltine. Some of these letters are preserved at Sharlot Hall Museum in Prescott today, along with a 1930 photograph of Jan and his large family in Hong Kong, which he had sent to Hazeltine.

On his return to China, Jan Con Sang sent this photo of his family in Hong Kong to his friend Moses Hazeltine in Prescott. *Sharlot Hall Museum.*

In 1937, the Second Sino-Japanese War began, with troops from the Empire of Japan invading and overrunning mainland China, which it maintained control of until 1945. The bloody conflict resulted in countless deaths, both military and civilian, during those eight years, and Jan Con Sang was one of the casualties.

An epilogue to this story: In 1989, Jan Con Sang's great-granddaughter Diana Cheng Yue and her family visited Sharlot Hall Museum and met with museum archivist Sue Abbey to see if they had any material on Jan's years in Prescott. The family was overjoyed at seeing Jan Con Sang's letters and photo in the archive's possession, and Sue Abbey would later write in a newspaper column about how memorable it was to meet them.

Today, the legacy of Jan Con Sang is carried on by his great-great-granddaughter Juliana Cheng on a Facebook page honoring his memory. This story remains a remarkable example of the past meeting the present.

On July 14, 1900, one of the defining events of Prescott's history occurred. A fire broke out and burned Whiskey Row to the ground as well as buildings on other blocks surrounding the Courthouse Plaza. The area was virtually all of Prescott's "downtown" at that time, and the loss was catastrophic. Historians are still debating the cause of the fire to this day, although the most prominent theory is that an overturned candle in a hotel room started the blaze.

Chinatown on Granite Street was only one block away from the conflagration, and while it sustained some damage, it was not completely wiped out. Why was this? Prescott's pioneer citizen Gail Gardner, one-time postmaster and prominent cowboy poet, discussed this in a recorded oral history he did for Sharlot Hall Museum. Gardner stated:

> *During the great fire, Chinatown did not burn! The Chinese got all their quilts and cushions and put them on the roof. Then they hauled water out of the creek and on to the roofs, and kept those things soaked all night long—all during the fire—and Chinatown did not burn in the big fire for that reason. You see, everything was drier than a cork leg, the whole town was, and sparks were falling all over the place. The town was built of wood, some brick buildings, but anything wooden with a tar-paper roof, why, a few sparks hit on it and it was gone. The Chinese knew that, and they covered their roofs with wet quilts. That was one thing, they stayed out there and took care of themselves—they knew what to do.*

Restored grave of Kim Toy in Prescott's Citizens Cemetery. Although little is known about Kim, there has been some contemporary interest in her as one of the few Chinese women whose name has survived in Prescott history. *Darlene Wilson.*

The burned-out merchants of Whiskey Row set up tents and shacks on the Courthouse Plaza in the ensuing days and continued business there while they rebuilt. In those days, there were no building regulations to prevent such a thing like there is today. Eventually, the downtown was rebuilt—this time with bricks and other less flammable materials!

THE MARCH 5, 1909 edition of the *Journal Miner* printed a very small obituary noting the death of a sixty-eight-year-old Chinese woman named Kim Toy. The notice stated that she was known in Chinatown as "China Mary" and that she had been in Prescott for around a quarter of a century.

Though the reasons are no longer known, Kim must have been fairly well known in Prescott, as it was highly unusual for the *Journal Miner* to run a death notice for anyone Chinese or of any other nationality. Because of this, she has attracted some attention from modern-day historians. In the early 2000s, historians Jody Drake and Parker Anderson sponsored her induction into the Sharlot Hall Museum's Rose Garden program, designed to honor pioneer women from Arizona who were here before statehood in 1912. This induction was to make her a representative of all Chinese women in territorial Arizona, since she is one of the very few whose name has survived.

Following this posthumous honor, a new headstone was installed at her previously unmarked grave in the Chinese section of Citizens Cemetery.

PRESCOTT'S CHINATOWN BEGAN TO die out during the Great Depression of the 1930s. There seems to be no defining single reason, but a lot of factors were at work.

First, it was the Depression itself, which ravaged the entirety of America. Many Chinese decided to leave Prescott to see if things were better elsewhere, others died off and, most significantly, Chinese immigrants were no longer arriving in Prescott regularly.

Second, as the Chinese either left or passed on, it remained a fact that there still were not many Chinese women in Prescott, thus not many children were being born. There had come to be a few Chinese families with children in the town, but even on Granite Street, they were a distinct minority.

This page: There are very few Chinese tombstones left extant in Prescott's Citizens Cemetery. Beyond this, there is little surviving physical evidence of Prescott's once-heavy Chinese population. *Darlene Wilson.*

By the late 1940s, they were all gone, and the *Prescott Courier* even proclaimed Chinatown to be just a memory.

There are some traces of their legacy yet. In a segregated corner of Citizens Cemetery in Prescott, there are still a handful of old tombstones with Chinese inscriptions. There are undoubtedly more Chinese burials in this corner in unmarked graves. When there were deaths in Prescott's Chinese community, they were buried locally, with their next of kin hoping to raise the funds to eventually disinter them and ship them home to China. A few succeeded, but many did not, and the graves are still here for the most part—at some point, probably in the 1960s, Sheldon Street was widened, wiping out four rows of graves in Citizens Cemetery, including a large part of the Chinese section.

In the early 2000s, the city of Prescott decided to build a large parking garage on Granite Street behind Whiskey Row to alleviate a downtown parking problem. To their dismay, they discovered that its location required under the law that an archaeological dig be arranged to recover any artifacts from Chinatown or the red-light district that might be buried there.

City officials and many townspeople were enraged by this requirement, seeing it as holding up progress on the much-needed parking structure. But the needed experts arrived, and the dig commenced. Scores of antiquated buried items were recovered, ranging from a fairly intact keg to various items of glassware.

By 2005, the parking garage had been built, and for a time, many of the recovered items were put on exhibit at Sharlot Hall Museum.

THE CHINESE LEFT BEHIND one other legacy as well, something they did not intend—legend and folklore.

There is a legend that sprouted up within the last thirty to forty years and remains very popular today. It contends that when they were here, the Prescott Chinese secretly burrowed an elaborate, lengthy and labyrinthian series of tunnels underneath all of downtown Prescott. The legend, when told, fails to explain how the Chinese of Granite Street, most of whom were itinerant, could have successfully excavated a lengthy series of structurally sound underground tunnels without attracting considerable attention.

Why would the Chinese have done this? Some of the legends contend it was to allow themselves the ability to get around town, that they were so hated by Prescott they could not leave Granite Street without being harassed and roughed up. Another, more racist, version of the legend says that it was so they could secretly surround Prescott and one day launch an attack, wiping out the white people and taking over the town.

The legend in virtually all of its forms contends that the Prescott city government today is engaged in a massive coverup of the tunnels' existence, although why the city would want to deny their existence if they are real is never satisfactorily explained.

The legend of the Chinese tunnels lives on as of this writing. There are two reasons for its endurance. First, most of the businesses of Whiskey Row and downtown Prescott were constructed with deep basements. These basements have been used, past and present, by business owners for storage. But basements are not tunnels. Prescott historian Patricia Ireland-Williams, in her book *Underground Prescott*, does an examination of these basements and speculates how they might have evolved into the popular tunnel legends.

(The old Moore's Laundry building on Montezuma Street, boarded up and condemned at this writing, has a basement accessible through a trapdoor that leads to what was clearly once a Prohibition-era illegal tavern, or speakeasy. The old bar and many other trappings are still extant, and there have been calls to restore this artifact and open it to tourists—but the cost to do this would be in the millions.)

The second reason the tunnel legends persist is more problematic. Whenever the subject comes up, numerous people swear they have been in the Chinese tunnels or played in them as children. Normally, when so many people attest to something, you would think that "where there's smoke, there's fire." Surely so many people could not be mistaken or lying about the same thing. In most situations, the present author would agree.

But the problem with this, in the case of the Chinese tunnels, is that not one person—not *one*—who swears to have seen the tunnels has, to date, been willing or able to provide any proof. When pressed for details on how to access them, they invariably back off or find some excuse for having a faulty memory on how they got in. Those who claim to have taken pictures and video of the tunnels have, to date, not publicly produced them. This is very significant.

The subject of the tunnels turns up on Prescott-area blog sites now and then. Following are several excerpts from blog posts on local websites from between 2010 and 2014. Some of these have since been taken down, but Sharlot Hall Museum has printouts of them:

Here's the deal people. 7 years ago, I read a report about the tunnels underground Prescott. Out of disbelief I flew there to squash these "tales." There are 2 entrances that have been blocked off in downtown to these tunnels. Only other way to get to them is through the sewage system. Call me sick but I don't care. Down there what you find will scare you. I found several skulls and other assorted HUMAN bones. I did not touch or take any of these back with me because of my respect for the dead.

The tunnels are true and were dug by Chinese labors [sic] *during the times when the Chinese were brought here to build the railroads. Chinese dug tunnels to move from area to area to prevent them from being beaten by those white folks. They also built their Opium dens where white people also went and paid for whores. This part of history was buried for the town of Prescott did not want the bad publicity. There is still a big cover-up. Our great grandfather has photos.*

I know from a reputable source that these tunnels do exist, and the person in question was recently in them. Not only that, but there is allegedly an entrance in the courthouse. The only way to get in them these days is to "know people" (or maybe use the sewer!!). This is a black eye on the history of Prescott, and the powers that be have tried to make its existence go away by covering it up. Way too many people have sworn that these things exist, while only a few biased parties claim otherwise.

The Chinese built the tunnels without the knowledge of Prescott people. But during the Whiskey Row fire, many of them were incinerated in the tunnels. In this day where there is still talk of paying reparations for slavery, Prescott could still be liable for this disaster. That is why the city has closed off the tunnels and are busy denying they exist. Look it up.

In the 1960's, I along with a handful of friends, explored the entire block just south of Whiskey Row and on the west side of Montezuma street, in a tunnel. There were names on the walls, garbage scattered about, and even some water wells dug here and there. Access was gained through an obscure trap door in an empty old warehouse a couple of doors down from Canarios [a bar].

Many Chinese were burned alive during the whiskey row fire in 1900. Back in the 80s, Prescott was warned they still faced liability for this, so they took action. They sealed up the tunnels, destroyed and shredded all evidence, and got sharlot hall museum to also destroy the evidence they had regarding the tunnels. This included every newspaper that made reference to the tunnels. This is why there are so many gaps in the supply of our old newspapers. Some were replaced with poor forgeries. But the coverup is crumbling.

There used to be several ways to access the tunnels, but over time some collapsed, some flooded, and the ones that still exist, well people don't want the liability issues, I guess. I know of an entrance close to Murphy's restaurant, one close to the Dinner Bell Café, one close to St. Michael's Café, one close to Prescott Jr. High track, another close to the Elks Opera house, even possibly close to the Court house. I won't reveal any directly out of respect for the businesses, but I do have VIDEO. I don't understand the denial past the liability issue, and there is definite resistance for some reason. Perhaps some families here in Prescott did some things in the past that would be considered immoral. Like killing the Chinese workers so as to not have to pay them for services rendered.

THEY DO EXIST! I have seen them with my own eyes, and I have VIDEO to prove it. Since I was about 15 growing up in Prescott, I went searching and went to the historical archives to find evidence. I was surprised to find how rude these people were when I asked about the tunnels. The more I looked, the more I found. They were partially exposed when the city built a parking garage behind whiskey row, they found evidence and artifacts which never made it into the public eye. Not sure what secrets Prescott is trying to keep hidden, but it's strange behavior without a doubt.

About twenty years ago, a friend of mine went exploring in the tunnels under Whiskey Row and they are there. But down around where Brick and Bones [a restaurant and bar] *is today, he found a piece of a human skull. It looked very old and charred, as if the person had burned to death. He called the police and was treated rudely and was told they would take care of it and that he had better not tell anyone else or he would regret it. The tunnels are real and the cover up is real too! My friend did determine that the tunnels ran along Granite street up all along Whiskey Row, and also went over to the Courthouse up to Cortez. He thought they went in other directions too. He saw some Chinese graffiti in spots too.*

Testimonies such as these, and many more like them, can sound convincing at first glance, until you realize a pattern with them. They all lack specifics—tunnel entrances are always "near" some landmark, without detail of exactly where. Those who claim to have photos and video never produce them. The person who could prove the existence of the Chinese tunnels would attract considerable attention; therefore, if they really existed, it would be inconceivable that no one would have provided proof up to now.

Because of this, as well as the logistical impossibility of the Granite Street Chinese accomplishing something of this magnitude without anyone noticing, the current author considers the tunnels to be just folklore. It is to be regretted that the legend shows no signs of dying out. But until/unless someone produces substantive proof, I cannot accept the legend as fact.

5

ATTACK OF THE PRESCOTT RIFLES

Nineteenth-century American towns often saw the formation of vigilante groups. In many cases, such groups operated under a shroud of secrecy, letting townspeople know they were around, but few knew the members' real identities. In other cases, such groups wanted more recognition and operated more openly. In almost all cases, though, these groups registered their displeasure with local law enforcement and vowed to take action into their own hands if they did not like the local officials' handling of town mayhem.

Around May 1882, a group of local men formed such a group in Prescott. Calling themselves the Prescott Rifles, they wore military outfits, had a stockpile of military-grade guns and ammunition and called their headquarters an "armory." Yet the Rifles had no official military affiliation. Some members likely were ex-servicemen and Civil War veterans, but they had no official military charter, nor were they connected to Fort Whipple.

Unlike many vigilante groups, the Prescott Rifles craved attention, and it was no secret who their members were. At formation, their captain was Frank Ingalls, while Will H. Johnston became their first lieutenant and J. Frank Meador was second lieutenant. Other members included prominent Prescott businessman Frank M. Murphy, Judge John A. Wright, Morris Goldwater (who would serve several terms as mayor of Prescott) and his brother Henry and store owner A.C. Burmister. There were thirty-two original members—a good start.

Early on, the Rifles realized they needed to make friends in high places, so at an early meeting, they voted to grant honorary membership to fabled jurist Edmund W. Wells, powerful businessman Levi Bashford and Charles W. Beach, publisher of the *Arizona Miner* newspaper. They likely felt that including Beach would get them good press coverage. But in the end, their coverage was only spotty—perhaps the *Miner* realized it was dealing with only a group of self-important men who liked to play dress-up.

The Rifles managed to obtain a meeting with Arizona territorial governor Frederick A. Tritle, accompanied by Secretary of the Territory Hiram M. Van Arman and Adjutant General Churchill. The territorial capital of Arizona had been moved back to Prescott at this time, and the government officials were easily accessible by groups such as the Rifles. After performing some military marching moves for the officials, Captain Ingalls requested that the Rifles be formally mustered in as members of the first regiment of Territorial Arizona Rangers. Governor Tritle, in what was likely more of a symbolic move to keep everybody happy, complied but added that he had no money to give them (which surely must have been a disappointment to the Rifles).

The months went on, and the Prescott Rifles kept holding meetings with much fanfare, but since Yavapai County law enforcement was efficient, there was little for the group to do. But in the latter part of 1883, ill luck started to befall them. First, in June, Frank Ingalls resigned as captain so that he could accept the job of superintendent of Yuma Territorial Prison in far southern Arizona. Then on October 20, the group was rocked by the sudden death of member George E. Ralph at the age of twenty-seven. The Rifles draped their armory in military colors for thirty days in mourning for Ralph.

On the night of November 22, 1883, the Rifles' armory burned to the ground. The building had been the former Prescott Opera House before the Rifles acquired it. It was a total loss; their guns and ammunition and other belongings were completely destroyed. The loss was estimated at $10,000, while they had everything insured for only $2,600. Local residents who supported the Rifles immediately began fundraising efforts, but it is unclear how successful these were.

Undaunted, the Prescott Rifles began meeting at Howey's Hall downtown, a building that was alternately used for meetings, social gatherings and theatrical performances. On or about May 21, 1884, the Prescott Rifles threw a big party in the hall to show the town they were still in business. Their friend Governor Tritle attended the soiree and gave a speech. After music, food and drink and some military marches, Mrs. Gorham Bray (wife of one of their members) formally presented to the Rifles a new American

Members of the vigilante group, the Prescott Rifles, pose for a portrait. Despite their uniforms and regalia, they were not an official military detachment. *From left to right*: George E. Ralph, Frank Meador and unidentified man. *Sharlot Hall Museum.*

flag to replace one they had lost in the fire. This flag was made of silk, with the name of the Prescott Rifles sewn across it.

In March 1885, the Rifles reorganized their officers. Patrick Ford, a Civil War veteran who had held a variety of Yavapai County positions, became their drillmaster. In June, they threw a large Grand Ball to celebrate the Fourth of July. It seems they also secured a new armory, but it is no longer known where it was.

Then tragedy struck. On December 20, 1885, Yavapai County deputy sheriff John M. Murphy was murdered by an itinerant farmhand named Dennis W. Dilda while trying to serve an arrest warrant on Dilda. Apparently, Deputy Murphy was a member, because the Rifles sprang into action. At last, they had some law-and-order issues to deal with. They spoke of storming the jail and lynching Dilda but ultimately did not do so.

The group placed a statement in Prescott's newspapers, which read:

> *It having pleased a mysterious Providence to take from us, by the hand of the assassin, our comrade, John M. Murphy, it only remains for us to put on record a tribute to his worth, and to express the grief of his comrades for his loss. While we sorrow for his untimely death, it is not for us to question the ways of Him who doeth all things well. In all his relations to us, as soldier, comrade and friend, John M. Murphy "wore the white flowers of a blameless life." By his death this company has lost one of its best members, the militia, a brave soldier, the territory, an honest and upright citizen and officer.*
>
> *In token of our sorrow for his loss, be it Resolved, that the armory and colors of the company be draped in mourning for sixty days.*
>
> *Resolved, that this preamble and resolutions be printed in the daily papers, spread on the minutes, and a copy sent to the relatives of our deceased comrades.*

When Murphy's body was brought back to town from Walnut Creek, where the murder occurred, the Rifles took charge of it. Murphy's funeral was held at their armory with large numbers of Yavapai County officials and citizens in attendance. Murphy was Catholic, so Father Franciscus X. Gubitosi from the Catholic church presided over the ceremony, after which a large throng of mourners followed the funeral procession to Citizens Cemetery, where Murphy was buried with a traditional three-volley gun salute provided by the Prescott Rifles.

Through 1886, the Prescott Rifles threw no fewer than four gala balls to keep their name in the public eye, but the clock was ticking for them. On

January 2, 1887, the *Arizona Journal Miner* newspaper reported on a rancorous disagreement at a company meeting:

> The Prescott Rifles have been peculiarly unfortunate in the selection of some of their committees. The poor shriveled up soul who takes occasion to vent his personal spleen at the expense of the company should be given a back seat in the social and business matters of the company. The denial of courtesies where due is not calculated to either make friends for the organization or to increase the friendship already existing, if the small souled specimen of humanity spoken of is continued in a position where he can place the company in a false light.

There are no further records of the Prescott Rifles after this notice, and it must be assumed they disbanded soon after. The reasons are unknown, but it was likely due to a combination of the infighting, as well as the Rifles' failure to really find a cause—a reason for existing—that they could sink their teeth into. Their presence in Prescott was slightly less than five years.

The Rifles did not have Prescott to themselves in what they were trying to accomplish. During the same period, another vigilante group formed in town that took on many of the same characteristics. They dressed in military uniforms, gave themselves military ranks (even though they were not an official military detachment) and boasted about what they would do if local law enforcement couldn't handle things anymore. This group initially called themselves the Milligan Guards but soon after changed their name to the Prescott Grays.

The group formed around May 1884. Not as much is known of them or their membership, although no man seemed to belong to both groups. Perhaps the Grays and the Rifles were rivals. At any rate, the Grays sought to curry favor from Governor Frederick A. Tritle as well. One of the first things they did was petition the governor to have themselves mustered in to the First Regiment of Arizona Infantry. This was denied, but in an apparent attempt to keep the Grays happy, Governor Tritle ordered Secretary of the Territory Hiram M. Van Arman to supply the group with one thousand rounds of ammunition from the territorial stockpile.

Membership seemed to be a problem for the Prescott Grays, as on April 17, 1885, it was announced they would present a medal worth fifty dollars

Members of the rival vigilante group, the Prescott Grays, pose for a portrait. Despite their regalia, they were not an official military detachment either. *From left to right*: William O. "Buckey" O'Neill (today remembered as a Prescott hero), W.S. Valentine and Jake Henkle. *Sharlot Hall Museum.*

to the member of the company who secured the largest number of new recruits. They also began having regular weekly drills on Friday evenings to perfect their military techniques. At one point, there was talk of staging a rifle shooting match between the Grays and the Prescott Rifles, but nothing came of this.

Taking a cue from their rivals, the Rifles, the Prescott Grays started throwing grand military-style gala balls at Howey's Hall to keep their name in front of the town. In 1885 alone, they threw such entertainments on May 6 (to commemorate their first anniversary of existence), July 4 and December 31. In April 1886, they challenged a group of Prescott baseball players to a game, but further details have not survived.

They threw another grand ball on May 6, 1886, to commemorate their second anniversary, and on August 21, they offered their services to the territorial government to go off and fight Mexican regiments during some border skirmishes (an offer that was clearly not accepted). They closed out 1886 with another ball, or "social hop," on December 9. The Grays must have disbanded shortly after that, as there are no further records of their activity.

Lawman William J. Mulvenon reportedly took possession of the Grays' guns and artillery after the group packed it in and broke it out periodically whenever the Yavapai County Sheriff's Department needed weapons for a posse. Later, in the early twentieth century, a local baseball team adopted the name Prescott Grays, but there was no relation to the vigilante militia group.

Today, despite a dearth of surviving information about them, the Prescott Grays are slightly better remembered than the Prescott Rifles for one reason. In July 1886, William O. O'Neill became their commander. O'Neill, whose nickname was Buckey, was editor of the stockman's journal *Hoof & Horn* at that time and went on to become one of the celebrated Rough Riders under Theodore Roosevelt during the Spanish-American War of 1898. Buckey O'Neill was killed in action in Cuba during that conflict and to this day is considered a major hero in Prescott history, with a famous statue crafted by Solon Borglum honoring him on the Courthouse Plaza. His one-time involvement with the Prescott Grays has caused some historians to regard the group as having been more important than it actually was.

6

HOW TO BE HORRIBLE IN PRESCOTT

Mardi Gras in New Orleans has been celebrated for many, many generations, and its key appeal is that men and (in more modern times) women dress up in outrageously garish costumes during the festival and, by their own admission, act ridiculous and absurd. It seems funny to imagine such antics being a part of the nineteenth century (since a lot of people believe the era was so stoic), but it actually was common throughout history in many parts of the world. But things like this didn't happen in small-town America—or did they?

In 1881, Prescott residents W.F. Holden and John F. Meador (very little is known about either man) decided to stage something memorable for Prescott's July Fourth celebrations. They and some friends formed a parade for celebration in which they named themselves "the Horribles." On July 4, 1881, at 2:00 p.m., they burst forth on the streets of Prescott, dressed in ludicrous costumes, singing wildly off-key, playing musical instruments badly (intentionally) and acting like they were on something a little stronger than alcohol. According to the *Arizona Miner* newspaper, which described the parade in depth, the head of the parade consisted of the "Horrible Fish-horn Band," followed by a man dressed as Satan. Then came a man dressed as Lady Liberty being pushed in a dump cart by another man.

On and on the parade went, with participants dressed as animals, historical figures, you name it. The *Miner* reported that it was "transcending anything in the line of burlesque display ever seen in Arizona." The Horribles then marched to the Courthouse Plaza, where they stopped,

The eclectic and offbeat entertainment group the Horribles march down Gurley Street in the 1880s *Sharlot Hall Museum.*

got up and read nonsensical pronouncements, like the "Declaration of Impudence," among other things.

The merriment was so original to Prescott that residents applauded the show. With this kind of reception, the Horribles decided to return the following year. In their 1882 July Fourth parade, they tried to outdo the ludicrousness of the previous year. Among many other things, a man portrayed then-president Chester Arthur, who was accompanied by a man dressed in stereotypical Chinese garb in a dump cart. Horribles members marched as Mephistopheles, Oscar Wilde, Uncle Sam and various Indians. At one point, a cart appeared with a flour barrel decked out like a mule head, with a body improvised out of a bird cage. As the Horribles had become popular after their debut the year before, the parade drew more respectable citizens to participate in the outrageousness—no less than the Prescott Rifles (see chapter 5) joined the parade in 1882, but as if worried they could lose respect, they were only willing to go so far as to wear white pants with yellow stripes.

The Horribles continued to march in Prescott on July 4 for years to come. Somewhere along the way, a man named Joseph Dauphin took over the group and was probably the most responsible for keeping them going. But while their marches remained popular with parade watchers, the newness wore off, and the newspapers stopped carrying detailed descriptions of what they did, often only noting their participation. When they were mentioned, Dauphin was usually noted as the man in charge. Very little is known about him.

Suddenly, in 1891, the Horribles outdid themselves. Their July 4 parade that year was highly praised by the *Arizona Miner* newspaper, which stated that the Horribles "eclipsed everything in this line ever attempted before in Prescott." The marchers were dressed as characters from *HMS Pinafore*—ostriches, elephants, an old woman carrying a man on her back, knights and Roman soldiers, and one man was dressed as a bottle. The public loved it.

Part of their renewed success might have been due to the Horribles having picked up a new seamstress, Zora Morgan, who worked hard for them and designed costumes that were beyond anything the group had ever dreamed of. Morgan (who was married to a local resident named Charles Morgan) was also the first known woman to have anything to do with the Horribles, although she never marched. Societal norms in those days did not allow women to publicly appear this way, though the parades did include men in drag.

Buoyed by the reception, the Horribles kept Zora Morgan as their costumer, and she continued to deliver for them, with the *Arizona Miner* singling her out for praise in 1893 and 1894 for her outfits in the parades. Her abilities drew some fame; in late July 1894, a group in Flagstaff contacted her and asked to borrow some of her costumes.

Above and opposite: The Horribles pose for group photos in their outrageous costumes, circa 1880–90s. *Sharlot Hall Museum.*

Zora Morgan died soon after, on October 31, 1894—fittingly, Halloween. Her obituary states that her body was shipped to Cambridge, Massachusetts, for burial. At this time, no historian has successfully located her grave, and it is likely that, over the years, it became unmarked (very common in many old cemeteries). As for the Horribles, there is no record that they ever marched again after 1894. Perhaps they were unable to find a suitable replacement for Morgan and decided it was time to pack it in.

Today, Prescott historians are fascinated by the Horribles and are frustrated that so little information about them has survived. Only a few newspaper articles and a handful of photos remain of their memory.

7

THE BEST PEOPLE ON EARTH AND THEIR OPERA HOUSE

B y the 1890s, Prescott had grown large enough to have a branch of virtually every fraternal organization in America, including the Masons, Moose, Odd Fellows and the Knights of Pythias. There was one notable exception—the Benevolent and Protective Order of Elks (BPOE, also sometimes referred to as the Best People on Earth) did not have a Prescott lodge.

After several years of discussion, appeals were sent to national Elks headquarters that there were enough potential members in Prescott to warrant the creation of a branch of the lodge in that town. Elks headquarters gave consent, and on January 28, 1896, Prescott Lodge no. 330 BPOE was born.

Elks District grand exalted ruler Ernest Ulman arrived by train from San Francisco to preside over the installation of the newly appointed officers of Prescott Lodge no. 330 and to initiate the thirty-six members who had been chosen from among Prescott's citizens to be the first Elks in Prescott. After performing the secret initiation and installation ceremonies at an undisclosed location, Prescott's new Elks convened at the Hotel Burke on Montezuma Street for a night of celebration, drinking and gourmet food. It proved to be a Prescott milestone—in the ensuing decades, Prescott lost some of its lodge branches. There are no longer any lodges for the Odd Fellows or the Knights of Pythias in town, for example. But Prescott Lodge no. 330 BPOE exists to this day.

But upon its creation, the Prescott Elks had not made any provisions for erecting a meeting hall, so they spent their first years renting other facilities to hold their meetings and events. But it was natural for them to dream of having their own meeting hall and lodge rooms, and finally, in August 1900, they decided they had enough money to do something about it. The lodge purchased a 50-by-125-foot lot on a hilly rise on Gurley Street for $2,000, and later in December of that year, they purchased another 50 feet of the lot. But probably owing to a lack of funds, construction did not begin right away.

In 1902, Prescott Lodge no. 330 formed an official Elks Building Association to raise funds to begin construction. The original blueprint by architect D.W. Millard was for a 150-by-100-foot lodge hall with two stories, at a cost of about $50,000. But things started to change when local businessman Frank M. Murphy announced he had purchased the old Dake Opera House just up the street and was planning to demolish it. This started murmuring among the Elks Building Association about possibly adding an opera house to the facility. After all, one of things the Elks lodge was known for in those days was building opera houses. Once upon a time, the United States was dotted with Elks Opera Houses. This is something the lodge does not do anymore.

The ongoing delays in construction resulted in the departure of D.W. Millard as architect, and he was replaced by John R. Minor, who promptly informed the Elks that he could add a grand opera house to their building for only an extra $15,000. Deciding this was a worthwhile endeavor, the Elks Building Association decided to raise the extra money by selling and subscribing stock in the new building. The citizens of then-small-town Prescott, excited by the prospect of a beautiful new opera house, happily purchased stock, and the money was raised.

By March 8, 1904, the site had been cleared and a concrete foundation had been laid. April 3, 1904—Easter Sunday—was set aside by the Elks to hold a large ceremony for the laying of the cornerstone of the new building. In those days, cornerstone laying ceremonies were fairly common for the construction of "important" buildings, often with various local trinkets embedded in the cornerstone. This construction tradition has largely died out and is seldom if ever done any more today.

The ceremony of the laying of the cornerstone for the new Elks building began at 3:30 p.m. on Easter (the time chosen to match the lodge's number) and consisted of parades, speeches and other fanfare. A delegation from Phoenix Lodge no. 335 came up from the south to participate. Once all of this pomp was over, construction began in earnest.

The Elks building was to be three stories high, with the opera house on the first floor, with four suites of retail space on the sides to be rented out to

Amid pomp and ceremony, the cornerstone for the Elks Opera House was laid on April 4, 1904. Construction on the elaborate building began soon after. *Sharlot Hall Museum.*

businesses. The second story, planned to be a mining exchange headquarters, ultimately remained vacant and unused until 1914, when the Elks leased it to the U.S. government to house the United States District Court for that area of Arizona. The third floor would consist of the Elks lodge hall and meeting rooms. For the opera house itself, Prescott Lodge no. 330 purchased $3,000 worth of theater scenery from the Chicago firm of Sosman & Landis, at that time the main manufacturer of theatrical scenery and equipment in the nation. A fire curtain made out of asbestos was also purchased—this was many decades before asbestos was revealed to be a dangerous substance.

Prescott Lodge no. 330 BPOE had hoped for a Christmas 1904 grand opening for the Elks Opera House, but construction delays made this impossible. Finally, they became optimistic enough to target February 20, 1905, as the grand opening date. The *Prescott Courier* newspaper ran a glowing article about the construction on February 6, 1905, with the proud headline, "Prescott's Present Pride and Index of the City to Be."

The Elks knew they had to have a huge attraction for the grand opening of the Elks Opera House. Somewhere along the way, they decided to shoot for the moon and go after the Florence Roberts troupe, a group of professional actors on the road with perhaps twenty plays committed to memory. The lodge had learned that Arthur F. Warde, booking manager for the Roberts troupe, was himself an Elk, and they leaned on him in the name of fraternal brotherhood to deliver Florence Roberts for the February 20 grand opening.

Florence Roberts is completely forgotten today, but in 1905, she was one of the best-known stage actresses this side of the Mississippi. She hailed from San Francisco, where audiences swooned over her for many years, and when she went on the road (under the sponsorship of San Francisco theater entrepreneur Frederic Belasco), she was one of the few women in America to be the head of a traveling theatrical troupe. Prescott Lodge no. 330 clinched the deal with Warde to have the Roberts troupe open the Elks Opera House with the play *Marta of the Lowlands* by Spanish Catalan playwright Angel Guimera. The play had been quite successful in New York two years earlier, and while forgotten in most of the world today, it still remains popular in Spanish Catalonia.

The grand opening was a huge success and went off largely without a hitch. In attendance that night, in one of the box seats, was notorious Montana mining magnate and U.S. senator William Andrews Clark and his wife. At this time, he owned most of the mining in the Jerome–Verde Valley area of Arizona (under the name United Verde Copper Company) and visited Arizona periodically to check on it. When the show was over, the happy audience went home, beaming with pride over Prescott's lavish new theater and convinced it would change Prescott for generations to come.

The Elks had originally planned to have a giant bronze or copper Elk stand on the roof of the building between two flagpoles. Earlier in 1905, Joseph McDonald, the vice president of the United Verde Copper Company, had told Prescott Lodge no. 330 that he would personally intercede with William Andrews Clark to have the company donate the statue. Clark agreed to have the castings made and, as a symbolic gesture, arranged to have the Elk made entirely from copper mined in Jerome. The copper was sent to a foundry in Ohio, and on May 31, 1905, the giant copper elk arrived in Prescott.

On June 5, 1905, under the supervision of building architect John R. Minor, the giant elk was installed on the roof, hoisted up by a block and tackle. Modern Prescott residents, historians and Elks lodge members have named him Bill. They contend he was named this from the beginning, but this is not documented.

On September 27, 1905, Prescott Lodge no. 330 BPOE held its first lodge meeting in the new building.

THE PLAN FOR THE Elks Opera House was to continue booking good traveling road shows and rent the building out for local events. But no one in Prescott Lodge no. 330 BPOE had any theatrical business experience, and they soon learned that operating a theater was not as easy as it sounded. Several lodge members came and went as managers in very short order, each apparently overwhelmed by the burden of the opera house. Overhead was higher than expected, and the lodge was blindsided by the poor quality of many traveling shows on the road, resulting in consistent audience disappointment. At one point, a top Elk promised Prescott in the newspapers there would be no more "tramp shows."

The theater turned out to not be the financial success it was believed it would be, and the Elks were sinking deeper in debt with it. While Prescott had train service, it was not on the main line between major cities—anyone coming to Prescott had to change trains somewhere or, in the case of traveling troupes and all of their people and equipment, had to charter a special train to transport them. The Elks had sprung for this extra cost for Florence Roberts but could not afford to do it for everybody. Consequently, many traveling troupes (especially the higher-class ones) refused bookings in Prescott, unwilling to pay the extra costs of traveling there.

The lower-class traveling acts that did come to the Elks naturally drew a lower class of audience. There came to be increasing incidents of heckling at performances, and in 1908, a brawl broke out involving drunken audience members when the theater management tried to throw them out. There were a few bright spots—legendary bandleader John Philip Sousa played the Elks in 1909—but a day of reckoning was coming for the Prescott lodge. The grand facility had been far ahead of what the little town of Prescott was able to give it.

By May 1910, the lodge was $42,000 in debt from losses on the opera house, and they knew they could not continue. Only five years in, "Prescott's Pride" was on the brink of closing its doors. After meetings and much discussion, Prescott Lodge no. 330 decided to get out of the theater business and lease the opera house to independent managers, who would take on all the responsibilities and headaches and pay rent to the lodge. Such a move was risky; there was no guarantee an independent manager would fare any better than the lodge itself had.

Stepping up to the plate was a man named Charles Howard, who had owned and operated a rival facility on the Head block of Cortez Street called

Exterior of the Elks Opera House, circa 1910. The building still stands and is one of the oldest continuously operating theatrical facilities in America. *Sharlot Hall Museum.*

the Electric Theatre, which specialized in vaudeville and motion pictures. As both of these entertainment mediums were very popular, the Electric Theatre had been siphoning off business from the Elks for the previous two years. After Howard secured the lease from the Elks, he closed the Electric Theatre and moved his vaudeville acts and movies up the hill to the Elks Opera House and reopened.

Some local historians have been disappointed to learn that the Elks became a vaudeville house only five years after it opened, and that the facility never really had a "golden era." But it must be remembered that this decision saved the Elks Opera House. We take motion pictures for granted today, so it is difficult to comprehend just how revolutionary they were in the early twentieth century—people never got tired of them. Plus, vaudeville is much denigrated by historians today, but it was very popular in its heyday. Thus, as Charles Howard reopened the opera house (now called the Elks Theatre almost exclusively), it started making money for the first time.

As a movie theater/vaudeville house, the Elks still underwent a high turnover of managers/leaseholders in the ensuing years, but it was doing

Earliest known photo of the interior of the Elks Opera House, circa 1910. After several misguided remodelings throughout the twentieth century, it was restored to almost its original appearance in 2010. *Sharlot Hall Museum.*

solid business. Around 1918, however, a significant change occurred, as Charles Born took over the theater. Born was a postman in Prescott and had also worked as an assistant to the Elks management for several years prior.

Charles Born was a natural showman, and he guided the Elks Theatre into its most prosperous period yet, remaining manager until 1942. After taking over, he scrapped vaudeville completely (it was starting to die out in America anyway), thus turning the Elks into a full-time movie theater, with occasional live acts here and there. He flamboyantly held regular press conferences to inform Prescott newspapers of everything that was coming. He started printing up weekly handbills advertising the theater attractions and hired boys to pass them out to pedestrians on the streets of Prescott.

Born also engaged in some theater remodeling in the late 1920s and early '30s, removing many of the steps in the facility and turning them into ramps for easier walking and reconfiguring the aisles in the balcony.

In 1933, an out-of-town businessman named Albert Stetson turned the old Goldwater mercantile store on Cortez Street into a movie theater—the

Studio Theatre—which was strong competition for the Elks. By the mid-
rs had fallen under the same management.

ed in 1942, Prescott businessman Claude Cline
tinued to manage the Elks Theatre until 1980,
longest-serving manager of that facility, a total

ts still have fond memories of the Claude Cline
my young people had first dates and first kisses
w many great films there. Ultimately, Cline
Prescott theaters that came into existence and
n movies in Prescott for many years.
made one decision that has not sat well with
winter of 1945–46, he had commenced a major
emoving all of the box seats and all of the lavish
l adorned the facility since 1905. Among other
s now strictly a movie theater and did not need
preservation of buildings was an idea far in the
as just an aging building, and no one thought
nodeling. It was not until after Claude Cline had
people started thinking negatively of his decision.
building was showing its age. Prescott Lodge no.
d its lodge rooms on the top floor those many
the decaying sixty-three-year-old building was
The members decided to sell, and after a couple
lding fell under the ownership of local attorneys
Don Head and Phil Toci, who moved their law offices into the second floor.
In the sale, the lodge had a stipulation that it could keep using the third-floor
lodge rooms until the group could find a new facility, and they finally vacated
in 1971, taking Bill, the copper elk from the top of the building, with them.
The attorneys continued to lease the theater to Claude Cline.

In 1980, Claude Cline retired, giving up his lease on the Elks Theatre.
Owners Head and Toci then made an agreement with businessmen Ronald
Swartz and Roger Pearsall to take over the facility, with the ultimate goal
of turning it back into a theater for live performances. The new managers
financed a new remodeling of the interior, adding a new antique-looking bar
to house the concession stand.

But for complicated reasons that are not entirely clear, Head and Toci
divided the building into two separate properties, condominium-style, with
the theater and lobby as one property and the upper two floors and lower-

level retail space as the other. Then they sold the theater portion to the Arizona Community Foundation (ACF), while retaining the remainder of the building for their law offices.

The ACF contracted with a newly formed group calling itself Prescott Center for the Performing Arts (PCPA) to take over management, with the intent of renewing live performances. During all of this confusion, the Elks stayed open as a movie theater, with *Raiders of the Lost Ark* becoming the final film to be shown there (in early 1982) in the facility's official movie theater period.

The PCPA had a lot of grand ideas and booked an impressive string of celebrity appearances for the Elks, including Kevin McCarthy (in his traveling one-man show *Give 'Em Hell, Harry!*), Vincent Price and legendary film director Robert Wise for a lecture. The PCPA believed advance ticket sales would cover the costs of these celebrities, but the populace of Prescott had other ideas. Prescott has long been a town that is not impressed by celebrity, and ticket sales were poor. McCarthy did appear, but most of the other performers canceled when PCPA could not pay them. This mortally wounded PCPA, and the Arizona Community Foundation evicted the group.

The lease for the Elks was then given to Yavapai College, which used the theater for its own needs, as well as renting it out to organizations who wanted to hold events there. When Yavapai College built its own auditorium on campus in 1992, it let go of the Elks lease, which was then given by the ACF to Prescott College, a small liberal arts college in town. It did the same as Yavapai College had done, using it for its own events and renting it out.

By the year 2000, local historic preservationists had become increasingly interested in restoring the much-decayed Elks Opera House to its original grandeur. In conjunction with this, Prescott mayor Sam Steiger (a former U.S. congressman) pressured the city council into purchasing the Elks from the Arizona Community Foundation as a first step in preserving and restoring the ninety-five-year-old theater. The City of Prescott now owned the theater, and it fell under the operation of the city Parks and Recreation Department, which continued to rent it out to groups for their events.

Simultaneously, famed historic preservationist Elisabeth Ruffner (who had long championed saving the Elks), along with Warren Miller (education curator for Sharlot Hall Museum) and other concerned citizens formed the

Elks Opera House Foundation, a group with the purpose of raising money to restore the interior to its original 1905 grandeur, or as close as it could come to it in the present day. Fundraising began in earnest, but the road was rocky.

By the turn of the twenty-first century, Prescott had become a much different town. Over the previous twenty-five years, there had been a huge increase in growth, and the city population increased almost threefold. For the first time, the transplants outnumbered the long-term residents in Prescott. Therefore, it was logical that the new people would have no vested interest in Prescott history or its culture, and they fiercely objected to their city tax dollars being used to operate an entertainment facility. They would show up at city council meetings to voice their displeasure. This change in Prescott likewise affected the fundraising by the Elks Opera House Foundation, and donations to restore the facility were very low. The situation was not helped by a much-publicized negative report from a financial institution that asserted that the Elks could never again become profitable and that it would operate at a big annual loss if allowed to remain open. Naturally, this caused Prescott's anti-tax protesters to demand that the city close the Elks immediately, tear the building down and use the lot for something more beneficial to the downtown.

In February 2005, the City of Prescott and the Elks Opera House Foundation partnered to celebrate the 100th anniversary of the opening of the theater. A week of festivities, including concerts and film showings, commenced, though attendance was below expectations again due to lack of public interest in the Elks. The week climaxed on February 20, when the Blue Rose Historical Theatre (a group formed by historian Jody Drake) performed *Marta of the Lowlands* 100 years to the night when Florence Roberts had opened the Elks with that show. Jody Drake herself played the lead as Florence Roberts had done. It was a significant historical event for the Elks Opera House.

In 2007, former mayor Jack D. Wilson arranged with Prescott Lodge no. 330 BPOE to return Bill, the copper elk, and he was placed on his perch on the top of building for the first time since 1971. A crane was used to hoist him up this time, as opposed to the block and tackle used in 1905.

By 2009, it had become clear that public donations were not going to save and restore the Elks Opera House. So, under the guidance of Elisabeth Ruffner, the Elks Opera House Foundation applied for and received a $1.25 million grant from the Harold James Trust, a philanthropic organization. With the money now secured to restore the theater, the Elks closed, and heavy construction began.

The box seats (gone since 1945) were replaced, along with Elkish decorations modeled after those seen in the old photos of the interior. New seats were put in, and all of the theater's equipment was replaced or overhauled. By the time the facility reopened to the public, it was beautiful. It was as close to the original 1905 look as current building codes allowed.

The fully restored Elks Opera House caused public and business interest to return. Audiences started attending in greater numbers again, and a higher class of groups began renting the facility, including two Phoenix-based groups that specialized in popular "celebrity impersonator" tribute concerts. The Elks Opera House had achieved what seemed impossible—a new lease on life.

In 2012, local philanthropist Ann Carson Dater and her daughter Andrea Smith (who had financed the refurbishment of the Knights of Pythias building on Cortez Street and turned it into the Tis Art Gallery) became interested in purchasing the entire Elks building to turn it into a full performing arts center, including the upper floors. Again, the building was turned into two separate properties in 1982, so the two philanthropists purchased the upper floors and lower retail fronts from the attorneys who still owned them and maintained their offices on the second floor. Then, Dater and Smith approached the City of Prescott government.

Despite the turnaround in business the Elks restoration had brought about, the Prescott city government was anxious to get out of the theater business and sold the theater portion to Ann Carson Dater and Andrea Smith. For the first time since 1982, the entire building was reunified as a single property. Work began in earnest to fully refurbish the upper floors into a full performing arts facility.

Today, the entire facility is known as the Elks Opera House and Performing Arts Center. The upper floors now consist of small performance halls, recording studios, a gala room, a dance studio and other accoutrements. It has been a hub of activity, although it was forced to close in 2020, like everything else, during the COVID-19 coronavirus pandemic, and it remained closed through 2021.

In 1905, the *Prescott Courier* proclaimed the new Elks Opera House as "Prescott's Present Pride and Index of the City to Be." It never fulfilled that lofty prophecy, but at the same time, the facility proved itself to be a survivor. During nearly 120 years of existence, the Elks saw many different incarnations, fell on hard times and nearly closed more than once but somehow always managed to bounce back and soldier on. It is one of the most historically significant buildings in Prescott and as of this writing seems to still have a good future ahead of it.

8

WHEN THE KU KLUX KLAN
CAME TO TOWN

One of the most enduring stories of Prescott is the brief history of the Ku Klux Klan in the area. The famed—or rather, infamous—white supremacist group has existed in various forms throughout America since Reconstruction following the Civil War. By the 1920s, the Klan was the subject of much public debate, with state legislatures and other authorities conducting investigations into killings, vandalism and general terror tactics attributed to the group.

The Klan had peak membership in the 1920s. This was due to a push by the group to start Klaverns (as their chapters were called) in small towns across the nation. In those towns, many of which had only very small Black populations, the Klan's efforts failed because they had very little to do. Many young men at this time joined not necessarily because they were unrepentant racists but because it seemed like the popular thing to do.

The first sign that the Ku Klux Klan had arrived in Prescott came on the night of October 23, 1922, when a huge cross was set ablaze on one of the hills overlooking the Government Canyon area. It was large enough to be visible to almost all of Prescott at that time. Prescott Klan No. 14 was born, but it did not exert much influence in the town in those days. The Black population was very small, so the Klan resorted to circulating pamphlets extolling its virtues and complaining about what it perceived as laxity on the part of Yavapai County officials in enforcing Prohibition laws. It singled out Yavapai County sheriff George C. Ruffner as the main target of this vendetta.

George C. Ruffner was sheriff from 1894 through 1898, in the days of train robberies, stagecoaches and horseback posses. Now, in his old age, he decided he wanted his old job back and was elected sheriff once again in 1922, in the time of automobiles and Prohibition-era bootleggers. It is known that as sheriff Ruffner did not support Prohibition and would often go as easy as he could on moonshiners. Prohibition is remembered with derision today, while bootleggers are remembered as simple men who sold illegal liquor primarily to feed their families during this period of tremendous economic depression. Sheriff Ruffner undoubtedly took all of this into account when forced by the law to go after them.

Prescott Klan No. 14 circulated a pamphlet around 1924, a copy of which is reposited today at Sharlot Hall Museum, that raged:

> *We receive many inquiries regarding law enforcement such as, why or by what authority does Sheriff Ruffner take upon himself the right to go out and destroy a bootlegger's still and turn the bootlegger loose? Was Sheriff Ruffner elected to office by the people to also act as Justice of the Peace, County attorney, Judge of the Court, and then tell the people he is saving the County money? Can Sheriff Ruffner prove to the people of Yavapai County that he has lived up to the oath of his office to the best of his ability?*

After more ranting and raving, the Klan pamphlet concluded:

> *All Klansmen of Prescott No. 14 take this occasion to recommend to the good people of Prescott that there is no better time than right now to clean up Prescott and Yavapai County [so] that we will be free of bootleggers and the vice conditions. To the bootlegger and dope peddler we have this to say: we are here to stay and Yavapai County is not large enough for all of us, so you may just as well make up your minds to leave or secure honest employment and be a real man or we shall do all in our power to see that you have free board and lodging with someone to watch you while you sleep.*

There is no evidence that Sheriff Ruffner responded to this tirade. As sheriff, he certainly knew that Prescott Klan No. 14 was not making the inroads in Prescott that it had hoped to and was not gaining any real influence.

By 1925, Prescott Klan No. 14 was frustrated by the lack of attention it was receiving, so it decided to do something flamboyant. One night, a group of hooded Klansmen marched into the First Baptist church while services were going on, handed the pastor a large white envelope filled with cash

The 1926 funeral march of the Ku Klux Klan parades down Gurley Street. They were making their way to Mountain View Cemetery (a considerable distance away) to bury their deceased member, Joseph Drew. *Sharlot Hall Museum.*

and marched out again without speaking a word. Along with the money, the Klan had enclosed a note that read:

> *We donate the sum of money enclosed herewith to be added to the building fund of your church. As you know, the principles of the nights [sic] of the Ku Klux Klan restrict their membership to those who accept the tenets of the true Christianity, which is essentially Protestant, and we hope you can find it consistent to accept this donation from men who serve and sacrifice to the right. To you and the good people of your church we extend all good wishes and our highest respect. Yours truly, Prescott Klan No. 14, Realm of Arizona, by Exalted Cyclops.*

In May 1926, Joseph Holsom Drew, a seventy-eight-year-old worker in the incinerator plant at Fort Whipple (the military fort that had been stationed near Prescott for decades already), dropped dead while working. Drew was the son of the slave-owning third governor of Arkansas, Thomas Stevenson Drew, and was a well-liked and popular worker at the fort. However, after

Graveside funeral service in Mountain View Cemetery for Joseph Drew, conducted by Prescott Klan No. 14. *Sharlot Hall Museum.*

his death, Prescott learned something about Drew that it had not previously known—he had been a member of Prescott Klan No. 14. In those days, Klan members never divulged their identities or the identities of other members. The only exceptions were made in death, providing the Klan chose to do so, and it did in this case.

Prescott Klan No. 14 decided to hold a full public Klan funeral for Joseph Drew. It even went so far as to buy ads in Prescott's two newspapers, the *Journal Miner* and the *Courier*, advising all members of the Klavern to attend. The memorial services for Drew were held at Lester Ruffner's funeral chapel, and then the funeral cortege, consisting of twenty-five hooded and robed Klansmen, left the service on foot and paraded down the streets of downtown Prescott in ritual formation, with the lead Klansman bearing an American flag. The procession was followed by the hearse and some non-Klan mourners. Local citizens massed along the streets, most of them attracted by curiosity, to witness Prescott's first (and ultimately only) Klan funeral procession.

The Klan marchers and funeral procession headed for Mountain View Cemetery, nearly three miles away. There, Joseph Drew was buried in his Klan robes, and in Prescott history, he is the only one truly known to have been a member of Prescott Klan No. 14. The citizens of Prescott undoubtedly knew, or could guess, who the other members were, but there is no surviving evidence.

Following this large public spectacle, Prescott Klan No. 14 disappeared from view. Deflated and perhaps financially hindered by Prescott's lack of interest in their cause, the Klavern just seems to have faded away. There are no records of any further Ku Klux Klan activity in Prescott after the funeral of Joseph Drew. There have occasionally been latter-day rumors of attempts to start a new Klavern, but to date, these are not known to have materialized.

The four-year presence of the Ku Klux Klan in Prescott has become a sore spot for some residents. Some area historians will not discuss it out of fear that it makes Prescott look bad. Some have even protested when the photos appear on history websites. And indeed, there have been instances where some individuals, frustrated by present-day Prescott's Rightist political makeup, use the Klan story as rhetoric against the town. But this is all much ado about very little. The Klan's presence is now one hundred years gone, it did not make much of a splash and it didn't last long in Prescott.

9

THE LEGACY OF *LEGACY*

lmost since the revolutionary birth of motion pictures, Prescott has been the site for on-location shooting of Hollywood movies. Scores of films have been shot in and around Prescott, perhaps most notably (or notoriously, depending on your point of view) the grassroots 1971 hit *Billy Jack*.

Prescott's first brush with filmmaking occurred in 1912, when the Lubin Studio came to town and filmed a number of its shorts. Lubin was followed in close succession by the Selig Polyscope Company, which did the same. Famed cowboy star Tom Mix got his start with Selig and filmed his first movies in Prescott. Charmed with the town, Mix would return from time to time after he became a big star to film more of his movies in this location.

But throughout cinema history, independent filmmakers with stars in their eyes have also appeared. They have fought hard to bring their visions to the screen independent of Hollywood, with financing from whatever sources were available and willing. Today, in the digital video and computer age, it has become much easier for such filmmakers to make their own movies, but prior to that, it was much more difficult.

In Prescott in the early 1960s, a local printer and former English professor at Arizona State University named Richard Snodgrass dreamed of being a filmmaker. He was strongly influenced by European surrealistic New Wave cinema that was starting to appear in American art house theaters. Moving into partnership with local photographer John Ludwig, a company called Counterpoint Productions was formed. Snodgrass began to fundraise to make his dream come true. He envisioned a four-part film he would name *Legacy*.

It is no longer known where Snodgrass raised the money, but it probably came from local investors. Prescott was still quite small in the 1960s—much smaller than it is today—and it still had a Mayberry-like atmosphere. It was still a town where everybody knew everybody else. The citizens were doubtlessly excited over the prospect of a completely home-grown feature movie coming out of Prescott.

A man named Dave Campbell was hired by Snodgrass to compose the film score. Actors were all locals who volunteered their services. The city government agreed to close off streets without payment, including the downtown, so Snodgrass could film scenes. Such a thing would be unthinkable today without a great deal of money put up to offset lost business to the downtown merchants. But then, small-town Prescott had gotten caught up in Snodgrass's dreams of a completely home-grown feature film being made there.

The only professional on *Legacy* was Ralph Luce, who was hired as cinematographer for the movie. Luce had previously directed a 1960 film called *Rebel in Paradise*, a documentary about the artist Paul Gauguin. That film had been nominated for the Academy Award (Oscar) for Best Documentary but had not won. It is unknown how Snodgrass became acquainted with Luce.

Richard Snodgrass began filming the black-and-white production as he raised money. The first section, titled "The Mannequins," was filmed in July 1962 and depicts a young boy overhearing his parents' divorce plans. He then wanders around town aimlessly while pulling a wagon. He starts playing with two discarded store mannequins, pretending they are his parents and eventually bashing them with rocks.

As Snodgrass continued to raise money, he filmed the second story, "The House," in February 1963. It depicts two little girls, one white and one Black, playing together and wandering into an abandoned house and accidentally setting it on fire. Afterward, both are scolded by their parents for associating with someone of another race. (A portion of this section seems to have been filmed at the Little Daisy hotel ruin in the town of Jerome.)

In April 1963, Snodgrass and his crew shot the most ambitious of the stories, "The Survivor." It depicts a little boy emerging from a cave and discovering that everyone else in town is dead. He runs around the streets of Prescott, surrounded by corpses everywhere. He runs in and out of businesses (including Prescott's legendary Palace Saloon), turning on the jukeboxes.

The implication, of course, is that a nuclear holocaust has happened. After all, in real life, this was the era of the Cuban missile crisis and the Red Scare.

The last segment, "The Family," was shot in May 1963. Little is known about its content, as Snodgrass would later cut this section for the film festivals he entered. Following the completion of shooting, he sent the footage to a California lab for a rush editing job, as he had already arranged to have the world premiere in Prescott the following month.

Original movie ad for the world premiere at the Elks Theatre/Opera House of *Legacy*, an independent movie controversially filmed in Prescott. *Author's collection.*

LEGACY HAD ITS WORLD premiere at the Elks Theatre (see chapter 7) on June 26, 1963, for a two-day run. The reaction of Prescott residents was one of general bewilderment to the surrealistic film. New Wave art house films usually did not play Prescott theaters, so the people were not used to this kind of entertainment, and many now had grave reservations about the movie that Prescott as a whole had sacrificed so much for.

The *Prescott Courier* ran an article on the controversy, noting that audience reaction had run the gamut from "outstanding" to "disgraceful." Then letters to the editor started coming into the newspaper. Leading the charge was the Reverend David Trimble, the rector at St. Luke's Church in town. Reverend Trimble complained of "at least three vulgar scenes which had nothing to do with the plot" and recommended they be cut before any further distribution of the film. "Unless this is done," he concluded, "I fear the good name of Prescott, identified with the film, will be hurt rather than helped."

The next day, a letter was printed from the other side. Patrick Henderson, a history professor at the University of New Mexico (who was visiting Prescott at the time of the premiere), wrote that he found *Legacy* to be "a sincere, moving picture."

The letters continued in the *Courier*. A resident identified as Mrs. F. Burge wrote, "I cannot understand educated men wasting their time with the thoughts that make up this film." Noting Snodgrass's background as an

English professor, Mrs. Burge stated that universities and colleges should be closed if this was the kind of mindset they were turning out.

The last word in the *Courier* was had by resident Sharon Allen, who wrote that she thought *Legacy* was "a great film" and opined that all of the "righteous indignation" showed how needed the movie was.

Of course, by today's standards, *Legacy* is very mild indeed. In 1963, no one had any idea of the excesses that were coming in motion pictures, as early as only a few years later, as movie censorship barriers started to fall.

RICHARD SNODGRASS PROCEEDED TO enter *Legacy* in film festivals, with the hope of picking up a national distributor who would release the film to theaters, probably on the art house circuit. For the festivals, he cut "The Family" from the film for unknown reasons, reducing it to a one-hour running time. In retrospect, this was probably a bad move, as films with that brief of a running time, then and now, have great difficulty in finding distribution.

Legacy reportedly won a Gold Prize at the Mannheim International Film Festival, as well as receiving a Directorial Citation at the Cannes International Film Festival for Youth. But these lesser awards did not cause distributors to go knocking at Snodgrass's door. In the end, *Legacy* failed to find a distributor, and to this day, it remains officially unreleased. As of this writing, it does not even have an Internet Movie Database (IMDB.com) page.

Richard Snodgrass never made another movie. In subsequent years, he would sometimes host revival screenings of *Legacy* around Prescott. Following his death in 1997, his family donated all of his *Legacy* material—photos, paperwork and celluloid prints of the film—to Sharlot Hall Museum. The donation included the rights to the movie, though at this time, the museum does not have any plans to do anything significant with *Legacy*. It does have VHS and DVD transfers of it, and anyone wishing to see *Legacy* can arrange for a screening of it at the Sharlot Hall Museum Library and Archives. As the film is almost universally forgotten, the museum receives very few requests for it.

10

THE RISE AND FALL OF THE SMOKI

There is perhaps no other story that represents Prescott in the twentieth century more than that of the Smoki (sometimes known as the Smoki People). They were a fraternal lodge exclusive to Prescott who exerted great influence in town for almost seventy years. Although the lodge no longer exists, bad feelings remain to this day, and their legacy is a polarizing one—many long-time Prescott residents have favorable memories of the Smoki, while younger generations who hear the story for the first time are dumbfounded that such a thing could have ever happened, let alone lasted for as long as it did. Likewise, Arizona's Native American tribes have bitter memories of the lodge.

It all started simply enough. Prescott lays claim to hosting the World's Oldest Rodeo, which has ostensibly been performed yearly over the July 4 holiday since 1888. Some other towns in America have disputed the claim, but generally, most rodeo historians have recognized Prescott as having the world's oldest annual rodeo.

But in 1921, mostly due to a post–World War I economic downturn, the rodeo had fallen on hard times and the City of Prescott was questioning whether it could continue to hold the rodeo. Soon, Prescott's business and civic leaders, including the chamber of commerce, came up with the idea to hold a large variety show at the county fairgrounds as a fundraiser for the rodeo. Titled the Way Out West Show, it would climax by having the business owners themselves come out dressed in Native American regalia and body paint and perform burlesque spoofs of the Indian tribes' sacred dances. These were the days when ethnic impersonations, especially for ridicule, were still considered "OK" by white society.

For the act, the Indian impersonators gave themselves the fictional name of the "Smoki tribe," the name being a pun on Hopi, though officially the pronunciation would become "smoke-eye." Some Prescott historians have claimed that the Smoki name did not occur until later on, but newspaper coverage of the Way Out West Show in 1921 clearly uses it.

The Way Out West Show went up at the Yavapai County Fairgrounds on May 26, 1921. Attendance was heavy, as many residents turned out to raise money to save the rodeo. After other variety acts, Prescott's merchants and civic leaders who agreed to participate in the Smoki dances came out in full costume, wielding bull snakes they had caught, and performed their parody of the Hopi snake dances and other dance rituals. The audience laughed and applauded—the Smoki had been the hit of the show.

The show was such a success that everyone decided to do it again the following year. The men had fun playing Indian, and it was decided that the Smoki should dominate the 1922 Way Out West Show. But with a year to plan, things started to change. The Smoki dancers started to take themselves seriously and saw bigger prospects.

At this time in America, the Indian reservations were under the control of the United States government and the Bureau of Indian Affairs. The reservations were not considered autonomous nations as they are today—in fact, many of them fell just short of being a type of prison system. For many years, the federal government had forbidden the tribes to do their sacred dances out of fear of tribal uprisings and rebellion against the reservation system. Though the tribes performed dances to their gods clandestinely when they could, it seemed to many that this part of Indian culture was dying out and would be forgotten by time.

Consequently, the Smoki group decided that for the 1922 show and beyond—they were already thinking about beyond—they would perform the Indian dances completely straight, with no burlesque intentions, including the Hopi snake dance, perhaps the most sacred of all Native American ceremonies. Thus, they reasoned, they would be preserving history—preserving Indian culture that might otherwise die out. It sounded very noble at the time, and the Smoki men undoubtedly were sincere in this belief. But in historical hindsight, one thing stands out—the tribes never asked them to do this, and tribal protests of the Smoki began early on but attracted very little attention in those days.

With these lofty goals in place for the 1922 show, the Smoki players had to figure out how to do the Hopi dances, as none of them had ever seen one. They enlisted famed painter/photographer Kate Cory for guidance. She had spent a number of years living on the Hopi reservation, photographing them and their rituals, and could coach them on how to do the dances. Likewise, local resident Marie Tumber had lived on the reservation for many years and knew enough about the Hopi dances that the Smoki recruited her to write them up and act as their choreographer. Both women were excited about the Smoki, believing they were playing a role in preserving a vanishing way of life.

In advance of the 1922 production, the Smoki asked local poetess and historian Sharlot Mabridth Hall to write up a publicity pamphlet for them. Sharlot was becoming increasingly noted for her work in preserving Arizona history and had served a term as official territorial historian in the waning days before Arizona statehood. Today, she is a legendary figure in Prescott history, with the museum she founded in 1928 now bearing her name.

Sharlot Hall wrote up a lengthy prose mosaic, describing the fictional origins of the Smoki, describing them as a truly mysterious Indian tribe who come and go at will almost supernaturally. With beautiful imagery and stylistic verbiage, it is the only piece of true fiction Sharlot ever wrote. The sixteen-page pamphlet went over big and garnered much publicity for the upcoming show. In 1924, she would also put the official Smoki emblem on the cover of the revised second edition of her poetry book, *Cactus and Pine*, as a tribute to them.

The 1922 Way Out West Show went over bigger than the 1921 production had, and the professional businessmen of Prescott realized they were on to something. Several decisions were made—the Smoki decided to continue to perform yearly, but they broke with the rodeo so they could keep all the proceeds for themselves. With this kind of income, they formed their own organization, which very quickly became a fraternal lodge, much like the Masons and the Elks and others. As a lodge, they adopted their own secret rituals, secret initiations and other such things as all fraternal organizations did. They never used the word *lodge* to describe themselves but referred to themselves as, of course, a "tribe."

Titles were bestowed on lodge officials, as all lodges did, with the head of the Smoki being granted the title of chief. Each member was to adopt an Indian-sounding name and was to solely use this name if speaking publicly on behalf of the Smoki. For instance, the Smoki's first chief, attorney Neil Clark, adopted the name of Clear Water. Members were required to get

Author and historian Parker Anderson stands outside the Smoki Pueblo building as it is seen today. It is currently used for public events by the Museum of Indigenous People. *Darlene Wilson.*

tattoos on their hands, beginning with two dots upon initiation into the lodge. The number of tattooed dots would increase the more a member was involved with the lodge, with a half-moon being added if the member rose in rank.

With the yearly Smoki show being so popular with the public, the Prescott Chamber of Commerce became heavily involved in promoting it. Chamber secretary Grace Sparkes was a heavy booster for Prescott tourism and was deeply involved with anything that would bring people to town. In 1925, she led a delegation of Prescott boosters to Washington, D.C., where they secured an audience with President Calvin Coolidge. On behalf of the Smoki, they presented him with an honorary membership in the "tribe" a red-and-yellow-banded Stetson hat and a tanned deerskin with inscriptions from lodge members and other prominent Prescott citizens. For the proud people of Prescott, all of this was exciting news.

In 1928, the Smoki added a women's auxiliary branch, as many fraternal organizations did. Members had to be approved by the men (of course) and

A Prescott Chamber of Commerce delegation led by Grace Sparkes (*center*) presents gifts from the Smoki People (including the large hat) to President Calvin Coolidge in Washington, D.C., in 1925. The Smoki also made Coolidge an honorary member of the "tribe." The other man in this multi-photo image is unidentified. *Museum of Indigenous People.*

Interior of the Smoki Pueblo lodge hall, probably taken in the 1930s, shortly after it was built. Although the Smoki are now gone, the building still stands, and this room is virtually unchanged. *Sharlot Hall Museum.*

were referred to as "Squaws." The elected leader of the women's branch bore the name of head squaw. (The term *squaw* is regarded as an offensive epithet today, but back then, no one thought anything of it.) Like the men, the "squaws" had to adopt Indian-sounding names.

HAVING BROKEN WITH THE rodeo in 1923, the Smoki lodge was able to keep all of the proceeds from its yearly show. With these, they eventually built their own lodge hall, on Arizona Street in Prescott, where they would hold their secret meetings, initiations, lodge parties and other fraternal matters. It was constructed to look like an old rock-hewn Indian pueblo, and in fact, they named it the "Smoki Pueblo." As the self-appointed preservers of Indian culture, they built a similar edifice next door in 1935 to house the Smoki Museum, a place where they would display genuine Native American artifacts, such as pottery, baskets, arrowheads and various things that had been plundered from Native archaeological sites (a practice fairly common in museums of the era).

As Prescott was then a much smaller town than it is today, it was easy for a fraternal lodge to gain influence, and the Smoki did. Many of Prescott's movers and shakers became Smoki members, and as such, the lodge had much say in the politics and direction of the town. Probably beginning in the 1930s through at least the early 1970s, if a man wanted to get anywhere in Prescott, he had to be a Smoki. If you weren't a Smoki, you weren't anything. It was said during these years that, in a way, the Smoki *was* Prescott.

The lodge became involved in other community events during the course of each year and engaged in many positive and constructive civic and charitable endeavors. They funded scholarships at Arizona colleges, and in 1944, at the height of World War II, the Smoki successfully raised $250,000 in E Bond sales (an enormous figure at that time) to purchase a B-24 Liberator bomber for the war effort, which had the name of the "Smoki People, Prescott AZ" emblazoned on its side.

The Smoki traveled to other cities in full Native regalia to boost Prescott by marching in parades. They were also a staple of Prescott's annual July 4 parade, which was never without a Smoki float for most of the lodge's existence. However, a negative reaction to them at a parade in Philadelphia in 1926 reportedly caused the Smoki to decide to stay in the boundaries of the state of Arizona.

The Smoki dancers perform in front of their traditional set at the Yavapai County Fairgrounds in this undated photo. They kept this up for sixty-nine years. *Museum of Indigenous People.*

The controversial Smoki snake dancers perform in this undated photo. *Museum of Indigenous People.*

But their signature event was always the annual show at the county fairgrounds, where they performed their Indian dances. Until their last years, their audiences were always packed, consisting of locals as well as tourists. The Smoki dances were heavily promoted to Prescott's tourist trade, and people went because it seemed to be the thing to do. An average Smoki show included some moderate dances, such as Native hoop dances and Hopi Kachina dances, but would always climax with their recreation of the sacred Hopi snake dance because it always got the audiences gasping and applauding. For months prior, the Smoki would prepare by going out and catching harmless bull snakes, often paying children to obtain the slithery critters. Although there is no real documentation, it was widely believed that the snakes would be partially drugged by ether or chloroform to keep them docile during the rehearsals and the actual performances.

The lodge boasted that their dances were well researched and as accurate as possible to the genuine article. This is a claim that has not withstood scrutiny. There is some surviving motion picture footage of the Smoki "ceremonials," and those who have seen them in recent years are virtually unanimous that the dances are not even close to a genuine Native American ritual. There have also been testimonies from Native Americans who attended Smoki shows saying that the dancers were terrible. The lodge members' Indian regalia (seen in surviving photos) has likewise come under heavy scrutiny in recent years, as the dancers recycled costumes from year to year, some wore exaggerated wigs and their body paint was much darker than the skin of real Native Americans—in fact, in some photos, the Smoki makeup looks not too far removed from blackface.

THE SMOKI LODGE HAD some prominent members over the years. U.S. senator and 1964 Republican presidential nominee Barry M. Goldwater was a Smoki before he entered politics. He was initiated into the lodge in 1941, narrated several of the Smoki ceremonials and himself performed in the snake dance in 1941 and 1947. After going into public service, Goldwater could no longer actively attend meetings, but he made it clear he always considered himself a proud Smoki. Sometimes when he posed for portraits, he held his left hand up in such a way as to show his Smoki tattoo. During his campaign for president in 1964, the Smoki voted to make him an honorary chief of the "tribe." They were, naturally, very excited by the prospect of a

A Smoki "snake priest" poses outrageously for the camera in this undated photo. *Sharlot Hall Museum.*

Smoki becoming president of the United States, but it was not to be. As we know, Goldwater lost the election by a wide margin to incumbent president Lyndon B. Johnson.

Another prominent member was Gail Gardner, famed cowboy poet and lifelong Prescott resident. He had been involved with the founding of the Smoki, and at the time of his death in 1988 at the age of ninety-five, he was the last surviving original Smoki. With his Smoki name of "Hair Lip," Gardner served as lodge chief in 1930 and participated in the ceremonials for forty-three years before age started to slow him down, but he remained a loyal Smoki for the rest of his life.

THE YEARS, AND THE decades, passed. The Smoki lodge was a Prescott institution with much political clout in the town. Every year, they would perform their annual show (or "ceremonial," as they called it) at the fairgrounds. Audiences and particularly tourists kept attending because the production was still being heavily promoted, along with the rodeo, as a signature event in Prescott.

To their detriment, the Smoki were oblivious to changing times. By the 1960s, ethnic impersonations in entertainment were slowly starting to fall into disfavor in America. Also, the Indian reservations were starting to be granted greater autonomy, thanks in part to a variety of court rulings. As the tribes became increasingly self-governing, this negated the Smoki's long-stated purpose of preserving Indian culture. Their efforts were no longer needed, if they ever indeed were. Still, the Smoki soldiered on through the 1970s. Audience attendance at the yearly show remained high.

Throughout their entire existence, the Smoki claimed they had the full support of the Native American tribes for their efforts. From a historical viewpoint, this claim is disingenuous at best. The Smoki dances were controversial from the day they started, and the Indian tribes, particularly the Hopi, did object strenuously. But in the early to mid-twentieth century, racial minorities had virtually no influence or access to the media, and their voices went largely unheard. The claim that they had the sanction of the tribes undoubtedly helped keep the Smoki going for as long as they did. Meanwhile, they continued to ignore tribal protests. Members of the Hopi tribe met with the Smoki in 1978 and 1980 to register their concerns, to no avail.

Above: One of the original Smoki founding members, pioneer citizen Gail Gardner (*left*), poses with Barry M. Goldwater (*center*) and Prescott businessman Russ Insley (*right*) at the Smoki Pueblo in November 1952. The occasion was a Smoki celebration of Goldwater's election to the U.S. Senate. *Museum of Indigenous People.*

Left: U.S. senator Barry Goldwater in his full Smoki regalia. This portrait was reportedly taken during his 1964 presidential campaign stop in Prescott, during which the Smoki named him an honorary chief of the "tribe." *Museum of Indigenous People.*

Undated later portrait of Barry M. Goldwater, sporting his Smoki tattoo on his left hand. This photo was used in his funeral program in 1998. A*uthor's collection.*

A turning point came in 1983, when freelance journalist Kris Finn published an article in the December 14 issue of the *New Times* (out of Phoenix), examining Native American grievances against the Smoki. The *Prescott Courier*, in Prescott itself, reprinted the article on December 18, 1983. It was the first major negative examination of the Smoki in its history, and they were not prepared for it. The situation was best summed up in a statement from Dr. Raymond Thompson, at that time the director of the Arizona State Museum in Tucson, who told Finn, "A bunch of white people working in isolation from the Indians and taking their sacred ceremonies and recreating them in their own fashion are really out of step with the way the world is looking at things today."

Reporter Finn interviewed a number of Native Americans for the article. Susan Betoney Schuster, a Navajo who had attended a Smoki show, told Finn, "I was laughing and angry at the same time. I couldn't conceive of people foreign to my people doing this. It is an insult." Mary Thomas, a Christian Hopi from the reservation, told the *New Times*, "If they had any respect for someone else's religion, I would think they would abide by their wishes and stop."

Finn stated in the article that a number of Prescott residents refused to talk on record about the Smoki out of fear of retaliation from the lodge, which still carried much weight in town.

For the article, Finn interviewed several Smoki members, none of whom acquitted themselves well. The Smoki chief was interviewed. He scornfully stated, "A lot of their young bucks will tell you the Kachinas are sacred and yet they'll turn around and sell you one." For all of the heavy research the Smoki claimed to do on Native American culture, the chief did not know the difference between a Kachina (benevolent spirits venerated by the Hopi) and Kachina dolls, which represent them.

Statements by other Smoki in the article were not much better. For many Prescott residents, the article represented the first they knew that the Indian tribes had been unhappy with the Smoki for a very long time. After all, the lodge had continued to state that they had the support of "most" tribal members. And so, the Smoki continued on.

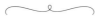

Many years of written protests and face-to-face meetings with the Smoki had accomplished nothing for the Hopi tribe. The lodge had rebuffed the Hopi at every turn, while still claiming they were honoring the tribes. The Hopi tribal government began to wonder if it was even worth it anymore to oppose the Smoki.

So, in 1989, the Hopi tribe sent several of its members to Prescott to attend and videotape parts of the Smoki show. This video was then screened for Hopi villagers, and afterward, the tribal government sent out a questionnaire to its members, asking for their opinion on whether or not it was worth it to keep fighting the Prescott-based impersonators. According to the tribe, the response was unanimous—stopping the Smoki needed to become the Hopi's top priority. But they knew they would need a new strategy; Native American tribes generally try to keep a low profile, even in disputes, but this approach had failed. They knew they had to go public—in a big way.

It was Saturday, August 11, 1990—Smoki day in Prescott. The traditional show was scheduled to go on that evening at the fairgrounds as usual. But early that morning, a busload of about fifty Hopi tribe members slipped into Prescott. They gathered at the Courthouse Plaza and spent much of the day in a protest demonstration, waving placards and signs with slogans such as "Hopi religion is not for sale," "preserve your own culture" and "free the snakes."

The Smoki were blindsided by the protest march and, in an astoundingly wrong-headed move, sent a Smoki named Eagle Claw (his lodge name) and four snake dancers to the Plaza to perform and try and counter the demonstration. Meanwhile, a Smoki leader pleaded with the protesters to disperse, inviting them to attend the show that night before deciding if it was disrespectful and sacrilegious. But the Hopi were having none of it; many of them *had* seen the show in previous years. That's why they were there. And they were not going to be put off and rebuffed by the lodge again.

That evening, the protesters gathered at the entrance of the Yavapai County Fairgrounds with their signs, handing out literature and asking attendees not to go in. Many people were shocked to learn the Smoki People really did not have the sanction of the tribes. Speaking of the demonstrators to the *Prescott Courier* newspaper, a senior Smoki member stated, "We believe this is a minority group. Not all the Hopis are against us—I've been invited to the homes of some of them. We're sorry about the misunderstanding, but….We have a 70-year tradition of our own."

The official Smoki emblem on the wall of the Pueblo. This image was used on all of the group's promotional material for virtually its entire existence. It was a variation of a traditional Hopi Kachina image. *Parker Anderson.*

THE WRITING WAS CLEARLY on the wall. It had been for a long time, but the Smoki had simply refused to see it. But on April 24, 1991, the Smoki chief that year, speaking to the *Courier* under his Smoki name of Pony Tail, announced that the lodge was retiring the annual ceremonial show and would not be performing it again. Speaking of the Hopi protesters of the previous year, Chief Pony Tail said, "If they don't like what we're doing, we're doing something wrong." By making this statement, it seems the Smoki wanted the public to think the Indians' objections were news to them, when this was far from being so. Later on, though, in an apparent gesture of defiance against the Native Americans they claimed to honor, lodge members would contend that the annual show was ended due to finances and dwindling lodge membership in the rapidly growing and changing Prescott, and not the protests. But nobody really believed this. The Smoki dances had been staged for sixty-nine years, 1921 to 1990.

Chief Pony Tail said the Smoki planned to regroup and were planning to organize new festivals in which they would invite genuine Native Americans to participate and perform. They also planned to invest more energy into their museum, located next door to their lodge hall, which had been displaying Indian artifacts since 1935 but was largely open only during tourist season.

The Smoki did arrange a few festivals for several years with Native American participants, many of them from other states where tribes were not overly familiar with the lodge's controversial past. These events were only moderately successful and did not last long. The lodge hung in there for a few more lurching years, but little was heard from them. With their signature event gone and reality long staring them in the face, the Smoki voted on April 1, 2001, to formally disband. Pony Tail was the chief that year again; he had overseen both the end of the dances and the end of the lodge itself. The members had one final steak dinner in their lodge hall, the Pueblo, and then they were gone. The powerful Smoki People, once considered the pride of Prescott, were no more.

THE LEGACY OF THE Smoki is a polarizing one indeed, and bad feelings still exist both ways on their memory. Longtime Prescott residents still remember the Smoki with much fondness and affectionately recall their many civic works and good deeds in town. Likewise, there are still a few surviving Smoki members left. They remain fiercely loyal to the defunct lodge, and are bitter about its demise, blaming their fate on "political correctness run amok." Reportedly, they will not even talk to historians about what the lodge's secret rituals consisted of. They feel that once a Smoki, always a Smoki.

On the other side of the coin, anger over what the Smoki did has only increased among Native Americans over the years. Today, the very name of Smoki is almost an obscene word to the tribes. They no longer even believe the lodge might have had good intentions in the beginning. To the tribes, the Smoki were a bunch of racist frauds from the get-go.

The present author believes the truth is, as usual, somewhere in between these two extremes. I can accept that the Smoki had the best of intentions when they started, believing they were preserving the dying customs of an indigenous people. I respect the charitable works they gave to Prescott over the years. But where they went wrong was letting their collective ego get the better of them and refusing to recognize and acknowledge changing times. By the 1960s at the latest, it had become obvious that Indian ceremonial rituals had not died out; an argument could be made that the Smoki mission was fulfilled by then. They should have packed it in at that time, if not before, but they stubbornly kept going because they were having fun and making money. If they had known when to quit, they might be remembered more favorably by history.

In 2015, a large bronze statue of former senator Barry Goldwater was unveiled in Statuary Hall at the U.S. Capitol in Washington, D.C. Standing over eight feet tall, the statue retains Goldwater's Smoki tattoo on his left hand.

But the greatest legacy of anyone or anything is always the legacy of unintended consequences, and this is certainly true of the Smoki. What they did had consequences far beyond the borders of Prescott. For many years, Native American tribes usually allowed non-tribe members, including the occasional tourist, to witness their sacred ceremonies and perhaps even take a photo or two, as long as they remained quiet, respectful and unobtrusive. This changed in the later twentieth century, as the Hopi and other tribes began to prohibit non-tribal members from attending their ceremonies. The tribes have also prohibited, for the most part, the taking of photos by tourists of virtually anything on the reservations without express permission. These bans remain in effect to this day, enacted as a preventative measure to keep the white man from ever stealing and misappropriating their culture again, as the Smoki had done.

The Museum of Indigenous People, formerly the Smoki Museum, as it is seen today. *Darlene Wilson.*

As an extension of this, the tribes in recent years have reportedly made requests of museums to destroy any photos they might have of Native American ceremonials, including the famous photos taken by Kate Cory and Clarence H. Shaw. (A museum archivist once told the present author that the Cory photos in particular had been requested to be destroyed by the Hopi tribe; her connection to the Smoki probably didn't help either, as the lodge undoubtedly studied her photos early on.) For the most part, the museums have refused, but as a compromise, they have enacted restrictions on the images so that researchers cannot view or use them without obtaining permission from the tribes.

DURING THE FINAL Years of the Smoki People, their museum became mostly an independent entity, and before disbanding, the lodge turned over most of its assets and property (including the Pueblo) to the museum.

The Smoki Museum reached out to the Native American tribes, telling them they wanted to take a different course than the lodge had done. The museum wished to continue to display Indian artifacts and history, but with the cooperation and input of the tribes. The response was cautious but positive, and in the years since the lodge's demise, the relationship has grown to the point where there are now Native Americans on the museum's board of directors, and in August 2020, the museum named its first Native American board president, Barbara Karkula, of the Citizen Potawatomi Nation.

For most of its existence, the Smoki Museum had been operated and staffed by volunteers—mostly lodge members and perhaps a few others. In September 1999, the board of trustees decided to hire a paid museum director, as other museums have. She was Ginny Chamberlin, an attorney with a bachelor of arts degree in history, history of art and business. Having a paid director changed the direction of the museum as well, as Chamberlin had no connection to the Smoki and could continue to help move the facility beyond the lodge's negative baggage.

Once the lodge was gone for good, the museum began to use the Pueblo for special events sponsored by the museum, and they sometimes rent it out to other groups for their gatherings.

In later years, the Smoki Museum began to open all year long instead of just in the summertime. It has been fairly successful and has hosted many fine Native American exhibits.

But despite its success as an independent museum, the Smoki name remained a touchy sticking point for many people, including Native Americans who had become involved with the facility. So, in 2019, under the watch of museum director Cindy Gresser, the board of directors voted to rename the edifice as the Museum of Indigenous People. As the last vestige of the Smoki name fell, there were objections from longtime Prescott residents, former Smoki members and descendants of proud Smoki. But by this time the controversial lodge was so far in the past that it made no difference, and the name change allows the museum to continue to grow as a business devoted to *genuine* Native American history and culture.

ALIEN THUNDER

Belief in unidentified flying objects, or UFOs, has always been controversial. The presumption has generally been that such crafts are piloted by alien beings from another planet or galaxy. Science has typically rejected claims that there could be life outside of planet Earth, though this has not stopped people from investigating. Likewise, many religious faiths (particularly Christianity) reject the idea that there is life on other planets, contending that human beings on Earth are the crown jewel of God's creation and that He did not create life anywhere else.

But UFOs remain controversial because of the many people who claim to have seen them over the decades. When seen, UFOs are variously described as saucer shaped or cigar shaped, and night sightings have been described as unusual flying lights that clearly are not airplanes or helicopters. Those who have witnessed UFOs are often denounced as liars or hallucinatory by non-believers. Conspiracy theories exist to this day among believers about a supposed coverup of their existence by the governments of the world. The subject has become so vast that no single book could give a comprehensive history of the phenomenon.

Although UFO devotees claim that documented sightings date back almost to the beginning of time, the subject really did not begin in earnest until the 1940s and 1950s, when an unusually large number of UFO sightings started to be recorded. This is when the media started to get interested. The very first of what would ultimately be tens of thousands of books and articles on the subject started to appear. Strange UFO religious cults, led by William

Dudley Pelley and George Adamski, sprouted up, attracting attention from a sensationalism-seeking media.

It should be noted that the term *Unidentified Flying Objects*, or *UFOs*, had not been coined yet in those early days of the phenomenon. Through most of the 1950s, they were referred to as "flying saucers." Naturally, Hollywood cashed in on the craze, and many science fiction movies depicting bloodthirsty aliens from other planets hit the movie screens.

Small-town Prescott, Arizona, was not immune. In fact, Prescott holds the dubious honor of hosting two of the most bizarre UFO incidents on record. After a number of residents reported seeing "flying saucers" themselves, the *Prescott Courier* newspaper assigned staff writer Mal Hernandez to write a four-part article on the subject, beginning on March 9, 1953.

Hernandez went right to the top—Prescott had its own flying saucer expert, George Hunt Williamson, who would become the focus of the entire series of articles. Williamson was an amateur anthropologist who had helped found the Yavapai County Archaeological Society in 1949, but he had later veered off into space alien research, joining the cults run by William Pelley and George Adamski. Williamson showed Hernandez plaster casts he had made of footprints from near Adamski's compound in Palomar Gardens, California, that he said belonged to alien beings.

As a side job to earn money, Williamson worked as an announcer at KYCA radio in Prescott. He told Hernandez that he began to believe in flying saucers while studying Indian lore as an anthropologist and found many references to strange objects in the sky among ancient Native American writings. He further stated that he himself had seen flying saucers on several occasions, the most recent being only a few weeks earlier, on February 3, 1953, when he and his wife saw three flying through the sky near their home at the corner of White Spar and Copper Basin roads in Prescott. Addressing his association with the controversial Adamski, Williamson told Hernandez that he had seen a saucer take off at Adamski's compound and that Adamski had conversed with the aliens, who warned him that the interplanetary beings were becoming increasingly concerned with Earth's experiments with atomic energy and nuclear bomb activity.

The *Courier*'s series got stranger by the day. Williamson told reporter Hernandez that he had a friend (who was not named in the articles) who was a short-wave radio operator and had made contact with space beings multiple times through his radio, using Morse code. Williamson claimed to have witnessed several of these sessions. His friend knew he was not being hoaxed by a prankster because he rapidly changed frequencies several times

UFO "channeler" George Hunt Williamson poses for a portrait at his side job as announcer for KYCA Radio in Prescott in 1953. The station still operates. *Sharlot Hall Museum.*

without ever losing the alien's transmission. Williamson provided Hernandez with a transcript he had taken of one of the conversations his friend had with an alien:

Q—Since you have space ships, how much more developed are you than earth?

A—Earth people think in years, we in terms of many of thousands of years.

Q—Are many celestial bodies inhabited?

A—Other bodies inhabited and in contact with each other,—Earth only one in solar system still isolated.

Q—We are told other planets uninhabitable because of gas and other conditions. Are your people like us?

A—We are the same as humans on earth. Scientists are wrong. Planets were created to support life, not made to spin in void while everything else created for a purpose.

Q—What power do you use in space craft?

A—Neither atomic nor rocket, but electro-magnetic, using magnetic lines of force much like planet in own magnetic field.

Q—How can humans live at speeds such as space craft are believed to reach?

A—Earth moves 1,000 miles per hour and earthmen do not feel it. We do not because operating in own magnetic field.

Q—How far has your medical science advanced?

A—We have no diseases.

Q—Why are you here? Why haven't you revealed yourselves?

A—Have been here several centuries. Have revealed ourselves to some people but do not want to interfere. Man must make his own advancement. Increased visits because of atomic activity and experiments with hydrogen bomb.

Q—What are we doing wrong?

A—Look to Nature's signs. Strange weather, floods, earthquakes. Earth is listing, unstable.

Q—Do you live in peace, have brotherhood?

A—Yes, we have followed Infinite Father; you have not.

Q—We have churches and worship God.

A—By word, not deed.

Q—What do you mean?

A—Thou shalt not kill, yet you kill.

Q—Why have you contacted us instead of the government?

A—Have contacted government. We do not have government as you do. Now people must also know.

Q—What is life like on other planets?

A—Similar to that on earth, but more active. Have art forms, music, and recreation.

With the historical hindsight of nearly seventy years now, it is almost certain that Williamson's anonymous radio operator friend who conducted the interviews was, in fact, Williamson himself. In later years, he would claim contact with spacemen himself, via radio and then via his Ouija boards. Plus, seventy years later, the above interview does not seem particularly significant in revelation and reads almost like a script to a science fiction movie from the era.

The *Courier*'s series ran from March 9 to 12, 1953. There must have been some negative public reaction, as they began running disclaimers on the second day, stating that the series did not necessarily reflect the viewpoint of the *Courier*.

As a postscript, George Hunt Williamson later left Prescott and began writing a series of books, first about UFOs, but later on, his views became more mystical. Under pseudonyms such as "Michael d'Obrenovic" and "Brother Philip," he wrote metaphysical books alleging that aliens helped create the Jewish and Christian religions by impersonating gods and passing on their teachings to man. He died in 1986 but remains a formidable figure in UFO research history. Most of his books remain in print to this day, and in 2016, a thick biography of him was published, titled *The Incredible Life of George Hunt Williamson*, by Michel Zirger and Maurizio Martinelli.

UFOS BECAME CONTROVERSIAL IN Prescott again in 1970. On August 3 of that year, the *Prescott Courier* reported that for the previous four evenings at the same time each night strange lights had appeared in the sky over Prescott. The lights moved back and forth and up and down, according to the reports. This would prove to be a prelude to a UFO event that was even stranger than the 1953 incidents had been.

After the article appeared, a self-proclaimed UFO "channeler" named Paul Solem contacted the *Courier* and claimed that he was in telepathic contact with the space aliens who piloted the crafts that had been seen, that

UFO cult leader Paul Solem speaks with twelve-year-old Dick Zabriskie in 1970 about the child's recent sightings of unidentified flying objects over Prescott. *Prescott Courier photo.*

he could summon the spacecrafts at will and that he had been responsible for the recent sightings over Prescott. Today, a man making such claims would likely be laughed out of the newspaper office, but in 1970, in the wake of continued UFO sightings over Prescott, Solem caught the attention of *Courier* managing editor Joe Kraus. Solem invited Kraus to his home one evening to witness himself calling a flying saucer to appear.

And so it was that on the evening of August 7, 1970, in the backyard of Paul Solem's home at 741 North Sixth Street, editor Kraus and several of Solem's neighbors gathered to witness Solem channel the space aliens and make their craft appear. According to Kraus, Solem stood off by himself for a while, mentally calling "them." Suddenly, Solem cried out, "They are here. I can't see them yet, but I know they are here. One just said, 'We're here, Paul!' There are several people in the saucer. I can hear them talking."

Then, according to Kraus, a large light appeared in the sky that had not been there before. It moved back and forth, changed colors from white to reddish orange to a purplish blue and then to a reddish white. The craft then moved and hovered directly above them. While it was hovering, according to Kraus, Solem repeated a message that he said was coming to him directly from the UFO:

My name is Paul the second, fourth in command of all ships that enter the atmosphere of the planet called Earth. We come to lend credence and as a sign or token that the Hopi prophecy was of a divine nature. Great sorrow and fear will be coming to this planet very soon and few will escape it. Our leader as spoken of in Hopi prophecy is already here (on Earth) in mortality as is known as the Apostle John (the same as in the New Testament). The white brother shall be introduced by a huge fire and the Earth shall quake at his arrival. We are of the 10 lost tribes and we will return several nights unless there is contempt for us.

Kraus was so overwhelmed by what he had witnessed that he, as managing editor for the *Courier*, put the whole thing on the front page of the Sunday edition of the newspaper on August 9, 1970. Kraus stated categorically that he knew what he saw and said that Paul Solem was either a hypnotist, a magician or telling the truth.

The *Courier* ran a sidebar explaining the referenced Hopi prophecy. The Hopi tribe believes that the human race will have three stages of life and that at the end of each stage mankind will be purified or punished depending on his acts. The last purification was caused by a great flood that destroyed nearly the entire world (similar to the account in Genesis). Hopi prophecy further contends that an all-powerful man known as the White Brother, outfitted in red, bringing with him Sacred Stone Tablets, will ultimately take control of the world and bring about the third and final Purification Day. The White Brother's arrival would also coincide with a great migration of Native Americans to the United States and Canada from Mexico and South America.

Solem blathered on to the *Courier* that the Book of Mormon teaches that the Church of Jesus Christ of Latter-day Saints holds "the keys," which they will turn over to the Native Americans as the end nears. He described the space aliens as looking mostly like humans, with hair to their shoulders and a musical tone in their voice.

"There is no reason to fear these people," Solem said. "They are like Angels. They come from the planet Venus and they are here only to lend credence to prophecy, not to harm anyone." Solem claimed that he had first been contacted by the saucers in 1948 while living in Idaho and that they told him he was the reincarnation of one of them who had lived on Venus.

Despite what surely must have been negative public opinion to the article, editor Joe Kraus carried on. The following day, he continued with more front-page coverage in the *Courier*, quoting local residents who had seen strange lights in the sky that were moving erratically the night before. Among those quoted was a Baptist minister, John Foster, who had been visiting Prescott from Phoenix.

All of Solem's talk about Hopi prophecy being fulfilled could not help but attract the attention of the Native American tribe, who sent a delegation to Prescott to visit Solem. Leading the delegation was the spiritual leader of the Hopi, Chief Dan Katchongva, who tribal tradition holds was divinely ordained (along with three other Hopi) to reveal Hopi prophecy to the public in 1946. Hopi tradition also holds that Katchongva was 110 years old at the time of his visit to Prescott. He was accompanied by aides and interpreters Ralph and Caroline Tawangyavma. Solem met with them immediately and offered to summon a saucer that night to give guidance to the Hopi leader regarding the final era.

The Hopi delegation quietly left Prescott within the next couple of days without making any statement about whether Paul Solem had successfully summoned a UFO for Chief Katchongva. But on August 18, Solem told the Courier: "The last day Chief Dan Katchongua [sic] of the Hopi Nation was here, the ship came in real low, about 800 feet." Solem made the statement certainly knowing that the Hopi tribe was unlikely to confirm or deny his statement.

While all of this was going on, Courier editor Joe Kraus had met another UFO researcher, Dan Carlson, from Chino Valley. Kraus ran an interview with him on August 11, 1970 (the third straight day of UFO coverage). Carlson stated that Prescott was favored with UFO activity and that a number of important UFO researchers had frequented Prescott over the years, including George Hunt Williamson and George Adamski, George Van Tassel, Truman Berthurum and Dan Fry. Carlson told the Courier, "If one is to believe Hopi Prophecy, the reasons the saucers are sighted here most often, and contactors seem to be attracted here is that this is a chosen land. Prescott is within the Hopi circle of sacred ground, where these beings from another world are supposed to bring about prophecy."

The Courier ran a photo given to them by Carlson, purporting to be of a UFO taken in 1963 near Albuquerque, New Mexico. The next day, Carlson had to fend off charges that the photo was a long-debunked fake.

On August 18, 1970, the Courier gave Paul Solem another front-page story in which he announced that his work in Prescott was finished and that he would soon be moving to the Hopi Reservation to assist them as the prophecy continued to be fulfilled. He planned a series of interviews on Prescott's KYCA radio before his departure. Meanwhile, the newspaper continued to

A delegation from the Hopi tribe meets with UFO cult leader Paul Solem (*standing left*). Seated is venerated Hopi spiritual leader Chief Dan Katchongva, who was reportedly 110 years old at this time. Right are Chief Katchongva's aides, Caroline and Ralph Tawangyavma. Prescott Courier *photo.*

print statements from residents claiming to have seen strange lights in the sky that could not possibly have been airplanes.

The *Courier* must have been receiving criticism for its ongoing UFO coverage, for on August 21, 1970, it gave the other side a chance to speak. Unidentified officials were quoted in an article as stating that the spate of UFO sightings could be attributed to satellites or weather balloons (the usual villains cited in debunkings). The article also quoted an unidentified source as stating, bizarrely, that a prankster had been flying over Prescott in a private plane at night, dropping hot air plastic bags containing a glowing substance and that this surely explained many of the UFO sightings—an explanation as difficult to believe as UFOs themselves. But Kraus remained convinced and closed the article with excerpts from a farewell letter Paul Solem had written to the *Courier*:

> *The coming of the saucers here and visual sightings were in confirmation of the Hopi Indian Prophecy. It was originally to your newspaper that I*

stated that they would make their appearance for several days. In fact, it was in the alley in back of the Courier *that the first ship made its pass to the bafflement of newspaper observers.*

Chief Dan Katchongua [sic] and Counselor Ralph Tawangyawman [sic] (of the Hopi) wish to thank those people who bore testimony as witnesses in their own personal way and to you who so generously gave time in publication of their Prophecy and verification of truth by those beings of another planet who allowed many sightings of their ships throughout the Prescott area.

In addition to this, the *Courier* ran a sub-article that day, quoting a local resident as having witnessed a squadron of large lights moving about over the mountainous Thumb Butte. The following day, the *Courier* ran another article quoting residents on strange moving lights they saw zigzagging around the night sky.

Then, all was quiet for a few months—until Paul Solem returned to Prescott in March 1971. He was accompanied by Hopi spiritual leader Chief Dan Katchongva, now reportedly 111 years old. Solem had been living on the Hopi Reservation since leaving town, giving consultation to Chief Katchongva about the imminent fulfillment of Hopi prophecy. (And presumably living off the tribe for his food and shelter; this did not mean the tribe all accepted what Solem was saying, but since Chief Katchongva had befriended him, they would not have had much choice but to tolerate Solem.)

Once again in Prescott, Solem made his most spectacular claim yet. He announced he would call down UFOs on April 11, 18 and 25 and May 3 to hover low in broad daylight at 2:00 p.m. each day. He chose a large field two miles east of the ghost town of Drake, far north of Prescott, and invited all residents to come and witness the arrival. Solem said he was arranging this with the spacemen because the sightings and events of the previous August had not convinced enough people that the coming of the Hopi White Brother was nigh. He blamed the mass media for ignoring him and the previous summer's sightings. Only the *Prescott Courier*

Paul Solem and Hopi spiritual leader Dan Katchongva on their return to Prescott in March 1971. Prescott Courier *photo.*

had given him coverage. Calling down the saucer in broad daylight would convince the skeptics.

On April 11, 1971, Easter Sunday, roughly 1,500 people gathered at the field near Drake to witness the promised UFO appearance. Solem was there, along with Chief Dan Katchongva. Solem had stated the saucer was fifty feet wide and would hover about one hundred feet from the ground and would be piloted by "Paul II" from Venus, as previously mentioned. A number of media outlets and radio stations arrived to cover the event as well.

At 2:00 p.m., Solem went through his motions of calling the UFO—but nothing happened. Nothing at all. By 2:30 p.m., Solem told a radio station that there would be a half-hour delay, probably because the spacemen objected to some "drunks with guns" who had shown up. After the drunks were routed, people waited some more. By 4:00 p.m., people started to leave, and by 5:00 p.m., it was over.

Solem angrily told the *Courier* that the UFOs did not come because neighboring ranchers were using bulldozers nearby to enlarge a water hole for their cattle. Solem claimed it was a deliberate attempt by the ranchers to sabotage the landing by destroying ground the aliens hoped to use. He said he was canceling the remaining dates he had set up for calling the saucers and would reschedule later.

It is very revealing that the *Courier*'s coverage of Solem's nonevent was not written by Joe Kraus but by staff writer Bill Parks, who treated the whole thing scornfully. Kraus must have felt like crawling in a hole—up until the day before the event, he had given Paul Solem much glowing coverage in the *Courier*. Now, suddenly, Solem's followers looked like fools.

Paul Solem disappeared from view for many years after that. He reappeared in the early 2000s, giving occasional UFO lectures in Idaho and Colorado. He died on February 11, 2012, in Blackfoot, Idaho, at the age of ninety-one. As of this writing, his memorial at findagrave.com states he was the only white man to be accepted by the Hopi. This claim is unreliable at best, because aside from his friendship with Dan Katchongva, it is not known how many, if any, in-roads he made with the tribe—especially after his predictions failed to come true.

As for Chief Dan Katchongva, he reportedly disappeared on February 22, 1972, at the age of 112. According to Hopi tradition, he stated that he was going to take a walk into the desert (from his home in Hotevilla, on the reservation) to meet a spacecraft. He never returned, and his body was never found. He remains a much-revered figure in Hopi tribal history.

Today, over fifty years later, it is difficult to evaluate the story of Paul Solem from a historical viewpoint. The fact that his many predictions never came true is ample evidence that he was a fraud, albeit a very convincing one. Also, the sacred prophecies of the Hopi tribe have not yet come to pass either. But there remain a lot of unanswered questions. *Courier* editor Joe Kraus was convinced he had witnessed Solem spectacularly summon a UFO in his presence. How Solem managed to completely convince the editor of this remains unexplained.

Likewise, Paul Solem's nonevent at Drake leaves more questions than answers. He surely must have realized the failure of a saucer appearing would completely discredit him, didn't he? So why did he do it? Possibly, like many hucksters throughout world history, he had become so immersed in his own rhetoric that he started to believe it himself. It is unlikely we will ever know for sure.

As of this writing, the world UFO phenomenon is still with us, with countless believers everywhere. But we are no closer to any solid answers than we were in the days of George Williamson and Paul Solem. If there is intelligent life on other planets, or in other universes, they have clearly chosen not to make any real contact with Earth—and certainly not in the manner that UFO "channelers" like Williamson and Solem described.

BIBLIOGRAPHY

Chapter 1

Barnett, Franklin. *Viola Jimulla: The Indian Chieftess*. Yuma, AZ: Southwest Printers, 1968.

Earliest History of the Yavapai Indians. "Indians-Yavapai." Sharlot Hall Museum Vertical File.

Yavapai-Prescott Indian Tribe website. www.ypit.com.

Chapter 2

Anderson, Parker. *Wicked Prescott*. Charleston, SC: The History Press, 2016.

McCormick, Richard Cunningham, and Parker Anderson, ed. "Days Past: An Arizona Governor's Memories of Abe Lincoln." www.sharlothallmuseum.org.

Munderloh, Terry. "Days Past: The Traveling Territorial Capital." www.sharlothallmuseum.org.

Patton, Barbara. "Days Past: Building a Mansion in the Wilderness." www.sharlothallmuseum.org.

Poston, Charles Debrille. *Building a State in Apache-Land*. Tempe, AZ, Aztec Press, 1963.

Chapter 3

Arizona Journal Miner, 1870–1907.
Goldwater, Morris, and Anderson, Parker, ed.. "Days Past: Arizona Territory's First Masonic Lodge." www.sharlothallmuseum.org.
"Organizations—Masonic Lodge." Sharlot Hall Museum Vertical File.

Chapter 4

Arizona Miner.
Lister, Florence C., and Robert H. Lister. "Chinese Sojourners in Territorial Arizona." *Journal of the Southwest* 31, no. 1 (Spring 1989): 1–111.
Tessman, Norm. "Prescott Underground." *Arizona Highways*, March 2004.

Chapter 5

Arizona Miner, 1882–87.

Chapter 6

Anderson, Parker. *Wicked Prescott*. Charleston, SC: The History Press, 2016.
"The Horribles." Sharlot Hall Museum Vertical File.

Chapter 7

Anderson, Parker. "The Elk That Roared: Memories of a Frontier Opera House." Unpublished manuscript.

Chapter 8

Anderson, Parker. "Days Past: A Brief History of the Ku Klux Klan in Prescott." www.sharlothallmuseum.org.
"Organizations—Ku Klux Klan." Sharlot Hall Museum Vertical File.

Chapter 9

Prescott Courier, 1963.
Richard Snodgrass Collection. Sharlot Hall Museum.

Chapter 10

DeWitt, Jennifer. "When They Are Gone." *Journal of Arizona History* 37, no. 4 (Winter 1996): 319–35.
Fee, Bruce D., and John D. Freeman. *The Smoki People*. Prescott, AZ: Smoki Museum Press, 2005.
Prescott Courier.

Chapter 11

Desmond, Drew. "1953: Prescott Is a Hotspot for Flying Saucers." *Prescott History* (blog). www.prescottazhistory.blogspot.com.
———. "1970: UFO Lands in Prescott." *Prescott History* (blog). www.prescottazhistory.blogspot.com.
Prescott Courier, 1953, 1970 and 1971.

About the Author

P arker Anderson is an Arizona native and a recognized historian in Prescott. He has authored the books *Elks Opera House* (with Elisabeth Ruffner), *Cemeteries of Yavapai County*, *Grand Canyon Pioneer Cemetery*, *Wicked Prescott*, *Haunted Prescott* (with Darlene Wilson) and *Arizona Gold Gangster: Charles P. Stanton* for Arcadia Publishing/ The History Press, as well as two self-published books, *Story of a Hanged Man* and *The World Beyond*. He has also authored a number of Arizona-themed history plays for Blue Rose Theater in Prescott